PEAK DISTRICT MARATHONS

by

JOHN N. MERRILL

Maps and Photographs by John N. Merrill

1987

A. J.N.M. PUBLICATION

a J.N.M. PUBLICATION

JNM PUBLICATIONS,
WINSTER,
MATLOCK,
DERBYSHIRE.
DE4 2DQ

Conceived, edited, typeset, designed, marketed and distributed by John N. Merrill.

First Published — December 1982
Reprinted 1983 and enlarged in February 1984
This enlarged edition — June 1987

ISBN 0 907496 52 0

Printed by: Commercial Colour Press, London E7 0EW.

CONTENTS

EARL STERNDALE

ABOUT JOHN N. MERRILL

John combines the characteristics and strength of a montain climber with the stamina and athletic capabilities of a marathon runner. In this respect he is unique and has to his credit a whole string of remarkable long walks. He is without question the world's leading marathon walker.

Over the last ten years he has walked more than 60,000 miles and successfully completed ten walks of at least 1,000 miles or more.

His six walks in Britain are —

Hebridean Journey	1,003 miles
Northern Isles Journey	913 miles
Irish Island Journey	1,578 miles
Parkland Journey	2,043 miles
Lands End to John o'Groats	1,608 miles

and in 1978 he became the first person (permanent Guinness Book of Records entry) to walk the entire coastline of Bitain — 6,824 miles in ten months.

In Europe he has walked across Austria — 712 miles, hiked the Tour of Mont Blanc, completed High Level Routes in the Dolomites, and the GR20 route across Corsica in training! In 1982 he walked across Europe — 2,806 miles in 107 days — crossing seven countries, the Swiss and French Alps and the complete Pyrennean chain — the hardest and longest mountain walk in Europe with more than 600,000 feet of ascent!

In America he used the the world's longest footpath — The Appalachian Trail — 2,200 miles — as a training walk. He has walked from Mexico to Canada via the Pacific Crest Trail in record time — 118 days for 2,700 miles.

During the summer of 1984, John set off from Virginia Beach on the Atlantic coast, and walked 4,226 miless without a rest day, across the width of America to Santa Cruz and San Francisco on the Pacific Ocean. his walk is unquestionably his greatest achievement, being, in modern history, the longest, hardest crossing of the USA in the shortest time — under six months (178 days). The direct distance is 2,800 miles.

Between major walks John is out training in his own area — the Peak District National Park. As well as walking in other parts of Britain and Europe he has been trekking in the Himalayas five times. He has created more than ten challenge walks which have been used to raise more than £250,000 for charity. From his own walks he raised over £80,000. He is author of more than seventy books, many of which he publishes himself. His next major walk — 2.400 miles — is down the length of New Zealand.

INTRODUCTION

Lying at the end of the Pennine Chain, the Peak District and Derbyshire, with its incredible wealth of scenic variety, has always been an area well traversed by long footpaths. Early this century, routes like the Derwent Watershed and Marsden to Edale became major challenges for the hardy walkers from Sheffield and Manchester, across the northern peat moorlands. The 1932 mass trespasses on Kinder brought walkers together before the second world war put a stop to marathon walking.

Since the 1950's there has been an immense growth of long walks all over the country - of which the Pennine Way is the principal landmark. During the 1960's I was flexing my muscles on my home ground, developing ideas such as the Limey Way and Peakland Way. In 1977 I did the ultimate walk in Derbyshire - 280 miles - around the whole boundary. Other walks in the last decade have been created by individuals, County Councils or by National Park offices. These include the Cal-Der-Went Way, Gritstone Way, Peakland Heritage Walk, and the disused railway lines of the High Peak Trail, Tissington Trail and Monsal Trail.

My aim in this book has been to collate all the major long walks in the area together. Not to give explicit details on how to do the walks, rather to give the necessary information about the route, maps needed and useful data. Several of the long routes have guidebooks to the walk, while others have little information. One of the attractions of a long walk, be it a 40-mile day walk or a longer multi-day walk, is the planning needed to do it. For several hours you will pour over the relevant maps and familiarise yourself with the route, problems and logistics.

In many ways people get more pleasure out of planning than actually walking it. Whatever you do, please ensure that you have good equipment, fit for the challenge, and that someone knowns your plans.

To complete my survey of the area, I have included routes such as the Staffordshire Way, Sandstone Trail and Gritstone Trail, which although on the fringes of the Peak District National Park are very much part of the scene. I have also included some new walks devised by mlself, which I hope will find favour with those seeking new routes. Although some of the walks are "challenges" to complete in a 24-hour period, there is no compulsion to walk them in a time limit. Walking is to be enjoyed, and, if you take 48 hours, who cares? The secret is to go out and enjoy yourself.

Since writing the above in 1982 many new walks have been created — several by me! As a result I have broadened the area covered by the book to include walks in South Yorkshire, Staffordshire, Cheshire, and Nottinghamshire, as well as Derbyshire and the Peak District. The number has now doubled to over fifty walks and I hope the book provides a useful guide to the remarkable variety of walking found in the northern Midlands. Have a good walk and I would like to hear from anyone who creates other walks not already covered in this book for inclusion in the next edition.

Happy walking!

John N. Merrill

WINSTER. JANUARY 1987

ROTHERHAM ROUNDWALK — 25 MILES

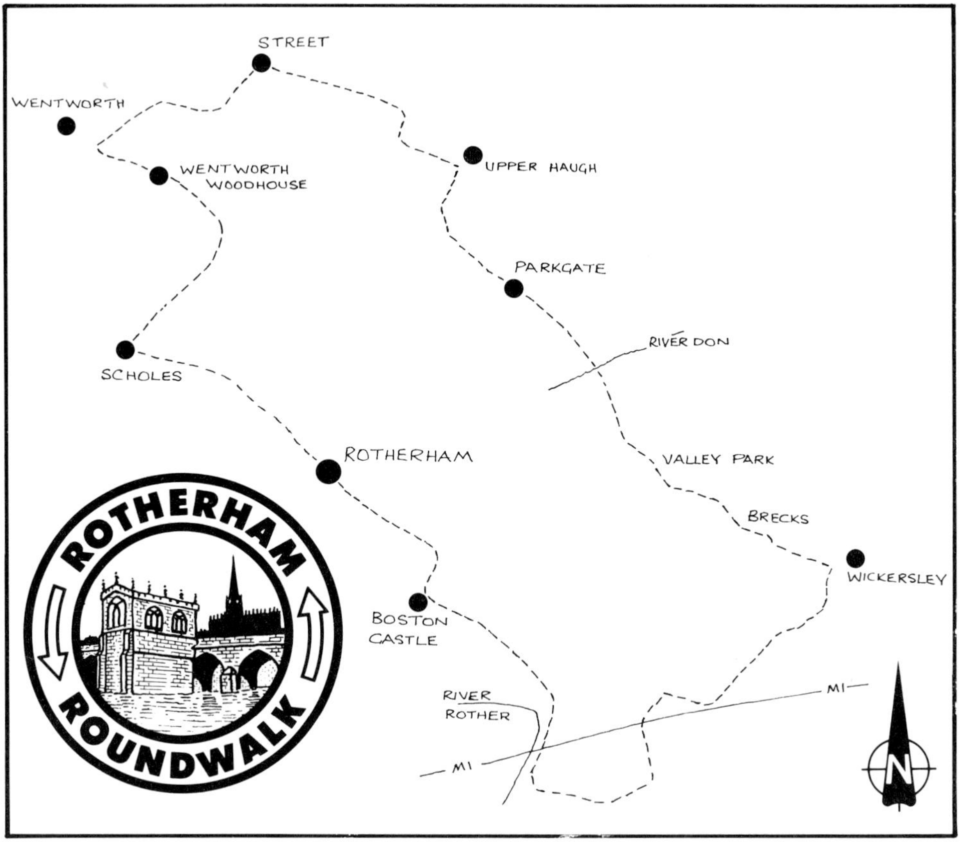

WENTWORTH WOODHOUSE

ROTHERHAM ROUNDWALK - 25 Miles - Circular

Developed in 1979 by members of the Maltby Rambling Club.

Although located in a major steel industrial area, the walk passes through very interesting countryside, past imposing buildings such as Wentworth Woodhouse and Boston Castle, and past churches and the rivers Don and Rother. In May an annual challenge walk is held round the route and through sponsorship considerable money is raised for a specific charity. In 1983 more than 700 walkers took part raising more than £5,000 for the Don Valley Body Scanner Appeal. Whilst 8 to 10 hours is usual for the circuit John Dowling holds the record; taking 4 hrs. 15 mins.

ROUTE OUTLINE
All Saints Square (Rotherham) - Scholes - Wentworth Woodhouse - Street - Upper Haugh - Parkgate - River Don - A6123 - Brecks - Wickersley - Pinchmill - M1 - River Rother - Boston Castle - All Saints Square.

MAP
O.S. 1:50,000 Sheet No. 111 - Sheffield and Doncaster

GUIDEBOOK
Rotherham Roundwalk by J. L. Ferns.

BADGE & TIME CERTIFICATE
From - Mr. A. Davis, 46 Gildingwells Road, Woodsetts, Nr. Worksop, Notts.

CHAPEL ON THE BRIDGE, ROTHERHAM

SHEFFIELD ROUND WALK — 10 MILES

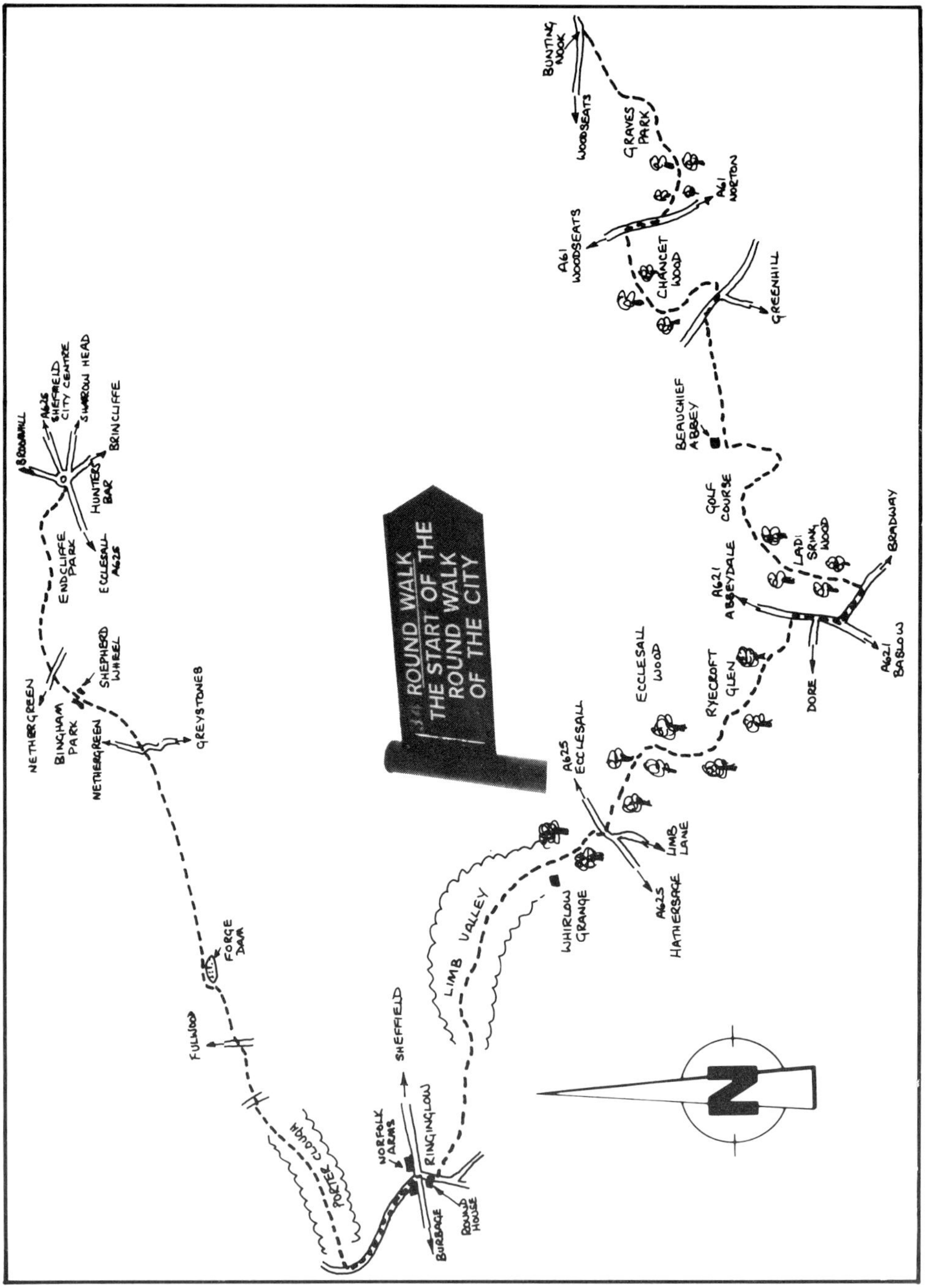

SHEFFIELD ROUND WALK — 10 miles

The walks' name is a misnomer as it is infact a horseshoe walk. The walks route lies on the western side of the city and is a remarkably attractive one within the city limits. First you walk close to the river Porter through parks and past dams with waterwheel's, the early days of the growth of Sheffield's industry. Gradually you ascend by the river through woodland and into unspoilt countryside as you ascend Porter Clough to Ringinglow, the highest point on the walk, 1,000 feet. Here you are almost halfway with a pub!

You descend the pleasant Limb Valley before entering woodland and begin weaving your way to Beauchief Abbey. Here you gently ascend to reach Graves Park, the largest of the city's parks, and gain Bunting Nook, the walks end. From here buses return you to city where another bus to Ecclesall will return you to Hunters Bar. Being in the city the walk can be done in stages using the cities transport services to return you to your starting point. I can highly recommend this walk and with parts of it being made in the 1930's it must surely be one of the first "official" walks in the country. The walk and history notes are amply detailed in the guidebook, and at all road crossings the route is well signed.

ROUTE —

Hunters Bar — Endcliffe Park — Shepherd Wheel — Whiteley Woods — Forge Dam — Porter Clough — Rininglow — Limb Valley — Whirlow Brook Park — Ladies Spring Wood — Beauchief Abbey — Chancet Wood — Graves Park — Bunting Nook.

MAP —

O.S. 1:25,000 Pathfinder Series, Sheet SK 28/38 — Sheffield.

GUIDEBOOK —

Sheffield Round Walk Sheffield City Council 1986

CAR PARKS —

numerous close to the route, and at Hunters Bar and Bunting Nook.

ROUND WALK SIGN

THE SHEFFIELD WAY — 45 MILES

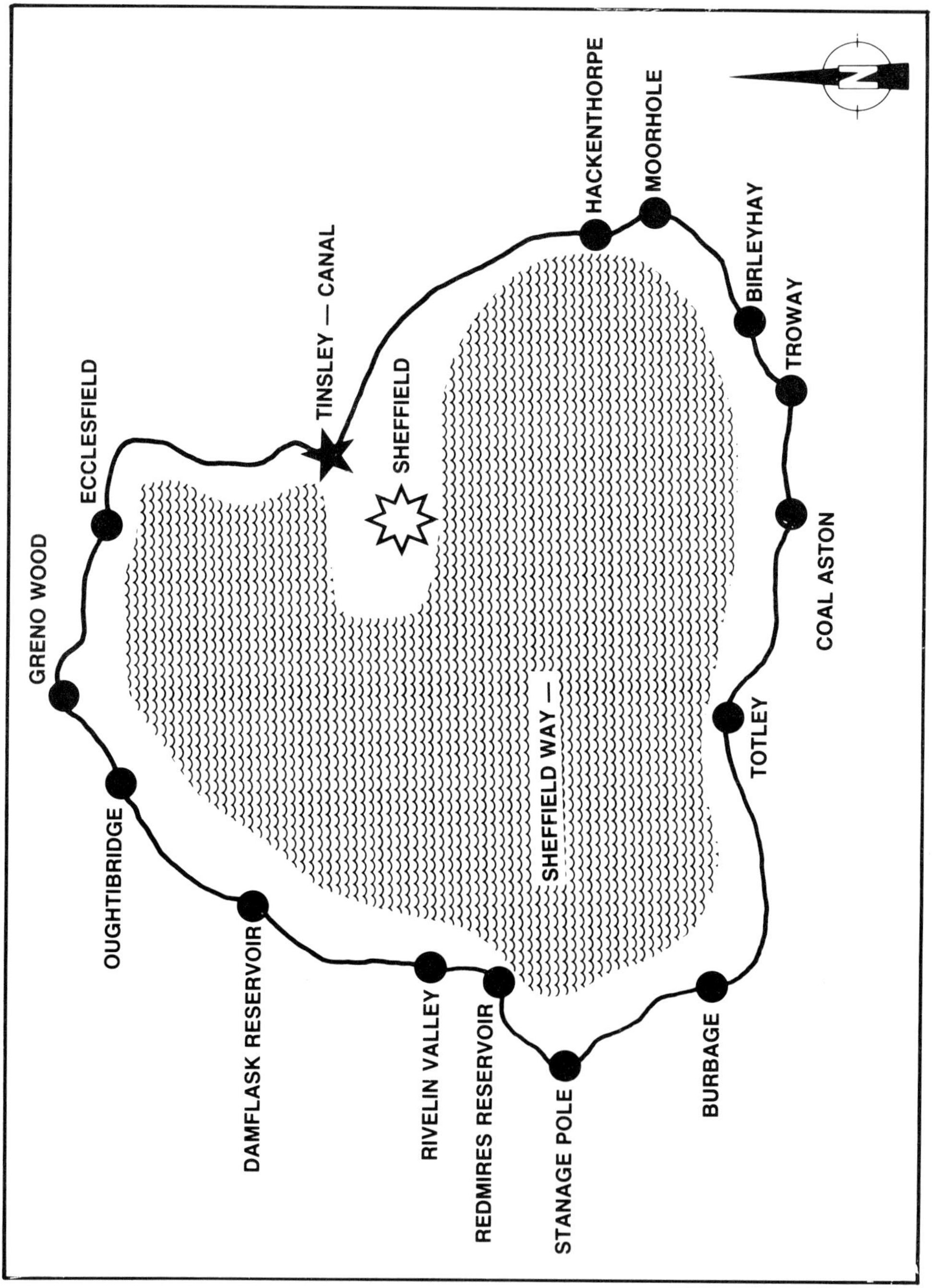

THE SHEFFIELD WAY — 45 MILES

— circular walk around the perimeter of the city.
Launch walk — June 30th 1985 — Time 17½ hours.

Sheffield is fortunate in being surrounded by woodland, moorland and on the western side by the Peak District National Park. This walk begins in the city at the Tinsley Canal, but you soon loose imdustry as gain attractive woodlands and gritstone outcrops. The route takes in the best scenery of the area including the Rivelin Valley, Stanage Edge, and Burbage. On the southern side are particularly attractive villages including Troway and Ford. The walk is usually done anti-clockwise and although possible to complete in a day — "far harder than the Lyke Wake Walk" — it best done over two days to really appreciate the walks splendour. The Burbage or Totley area make a good half way halt, with transport back to the city for overnight accomodation.

ROUTE —

Tinsley Canal at Wharf Lane — Canal — River Don — Hill Top — Thundercliffe — Butterthwaite — Ecclesfield — Whitley — Greno Wood — Wharncliffe — Oughtibridge — Loxley Chase — Damflask Reservoir — Hill Top — Rivelin Valley — Redmires Reservoir — Stanage Pole — Burbage Moor — Stony Ridge — Totley — Woodthorpe Hall — Mickley — Birchitt — Coal Aston — Troway — Birleyhay — Ford — Plumbley — Mosbrough Moor — Moorhole — Hackenthorpe — Woodhouse — Handsworth — Tinsley Park Golf Course — Tinsley Canal.

MAPS —

O.S. 1:50,000 Sheet No 110 — Sheffield and Huddersfield
O.S. 1:50,000 Sheet No 111 — Sheffield & Doncaster area
O.S. 1:50,000 Sheet No 119 — Buxton, Matlock and Dove Dale
O.S. 1:25,000 Outdoor Leisure Map — The White Peak — East Sheet
O.S. 1:25,000 Sheet No SK 29/39 — Sheffield (North) & Stocksbridge
O.S. 1:25,000 Sheet No SK 28/38 — Sheffield
O.S. 1:25,000 Sheet No SK 27/37 — Dronfield

GUIDEBOOK —

The Sheffield Way Peter Price Sheffield City Libraries 1986.

STANAGE EDGE & MILLSTONES

THE CAL-DER-WENT WALK — 30 MILES

HOWDEN RESERVOIR

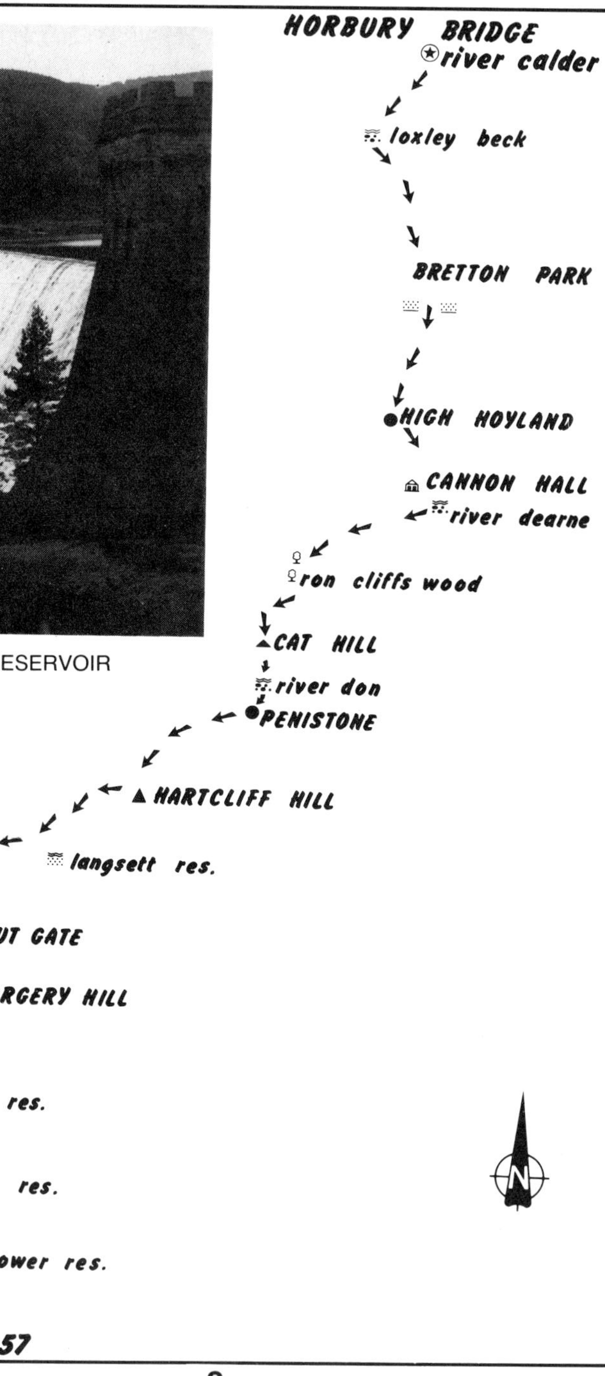

THE CAL-DER-WENT WALK - 30 Miles

From the River Calder to the River Derwent

Inaugural walk - May 20th 1978 by 15 walkers from the St. John's Methodist Church Lyke Wake Club, Ossett, in 11 hrs. and 20 minutes.

I first did this walk in March 1980 in 10 hours, walking from north to south. I found it a delightful walk through pleasant rural scenery, crossing the Calder, Dearne, Don and Porter river valleys to the Derwent. Being easily accessible, the support party had no problems contacting the walking party. The hardest part is the last twelve miles across the peat moorland near Margery Hill to Ladybower Reservoir. But it is all worth it - a really enjoyable day "challenge" walk.

ROUTE OUTLINE
Horbury Bridge - A636 - Bretton Lakes - River Dearne - High Hoyland - Cannon Hall - Rons Cliff Wood - Cat Hill - River Don - Bank House Farm - Hartcliff Hill - River Porter - Cut Gate - River Derwent - Howden Reservoir - Derwent Reservoir - Ladybower Reservoir - A57.

MAPS
1:50,000 O.S. Sheet No. 110 - Sheffield and Huddersfield - whole route.
1:25,000 O.S. Outdoor Leisure Map - The Dark Peak - southern half.

GUIDEBOOK
The Cal-Der-Went Walk by Geoffrey Carr. Dalesman 1979.

BADGES & COMPLETION CARDS
The 'Cal-der-Went Walk' Recorder, Fern Cottage, Cardigan Lane, Manor Road, Ossett, West Yorkshire.

ACCOMODATION
Youth Hostel - Langsett.

GROUP GETTING READY TO START WALK

CANNON HALL

LADYBOWER RESERVOIR

CRESWELL CRAGS

ARCHWAY HOUSE, NEAR EDWINSTOWE

THE LITTLE JOHN CHALLENGE WALK — 28 MILES

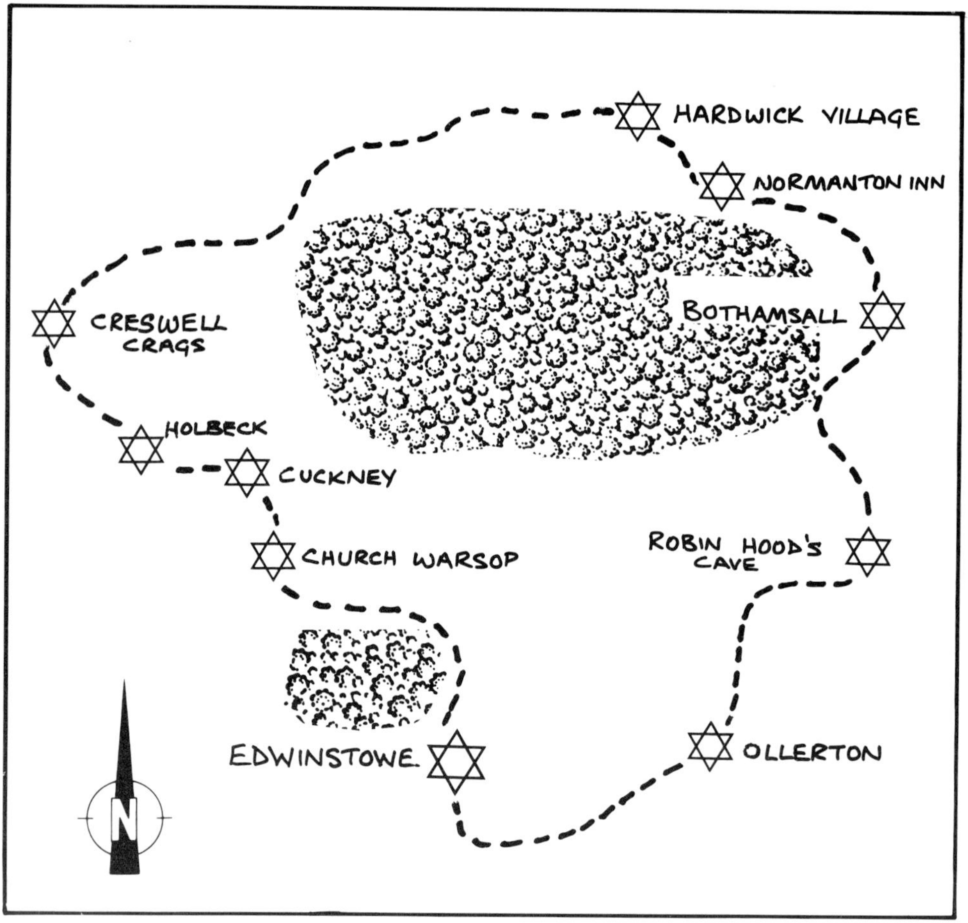

CONJURE ALDERS

THE LITTLE JOHN CHALLENGE WALK — 28 MILES

Inaugurated by John N. Merrill on July 5th 1986

A continuation of the Challenge walks devised and created by John Merrill. In 1985 he published a walk guide to the Dukeries area. From these walks he gathered together his favourite places and joined them into one long walk, keeping to as much forest as possible. The walk explores the fabled Robin Hood country and several places associated with the legend are passed or just off the route. Slightly longer than his other challenge walks but being flat countryside he felt this was alright and well within the average person's capabilities to complete in a day or over a weekend. The walks includes many of the key features of the Dukeries and Sherwood Forest area and is an indication of the excellent walking to be found in this area of Nottinghamshire.

ROUTE —

Edwinstowe — Budby South Forest — Church Warsop — Oakfield Plantation — Cuckney — Welbeck Park — Holbeck — Creswell Crags — Welbeck Park — Duchess Plantation — Truman's Lodge — Clumber Park — Hardwick Village — Normanton Inn — Bothamsall — Conjure Alders — Robin Hood's Cave — Whitewater Bridge — Ollerton — Edwinstowe.

MAPS –

— O.S. 1;50,000 Sheet No 120 — Mansfield & Worksop area
— O.S. 1:25,000 Pathfinder series — Sheet SK66/76 — Ollerton
— Sheet SK46/56 — Mansfield North
— Sheet SK47/57 — Worksop (South) & Stavely
— Sheet SK67/77 — Clumber Park & East Markham

GUIDEBOOK —

The Little John Challenge by John N. Merrill. JNM PUBLICATIONS 1986

BADGES AND COMPLETION CERTIFICATE — from JNM Publications

ACCOMODATION —

Camping — Edwinstowe
Hotels/Bed & breakfast — Edwinstowe, Cuckney, & Ollerton
Inns — six along the route at Cuckney, Clumber, Ollerton and Edwinstowe.

LITTLE JOHN'S GRAVE, HATHERSAGE

THE ROBIN HOOD WAY — 88 MILES

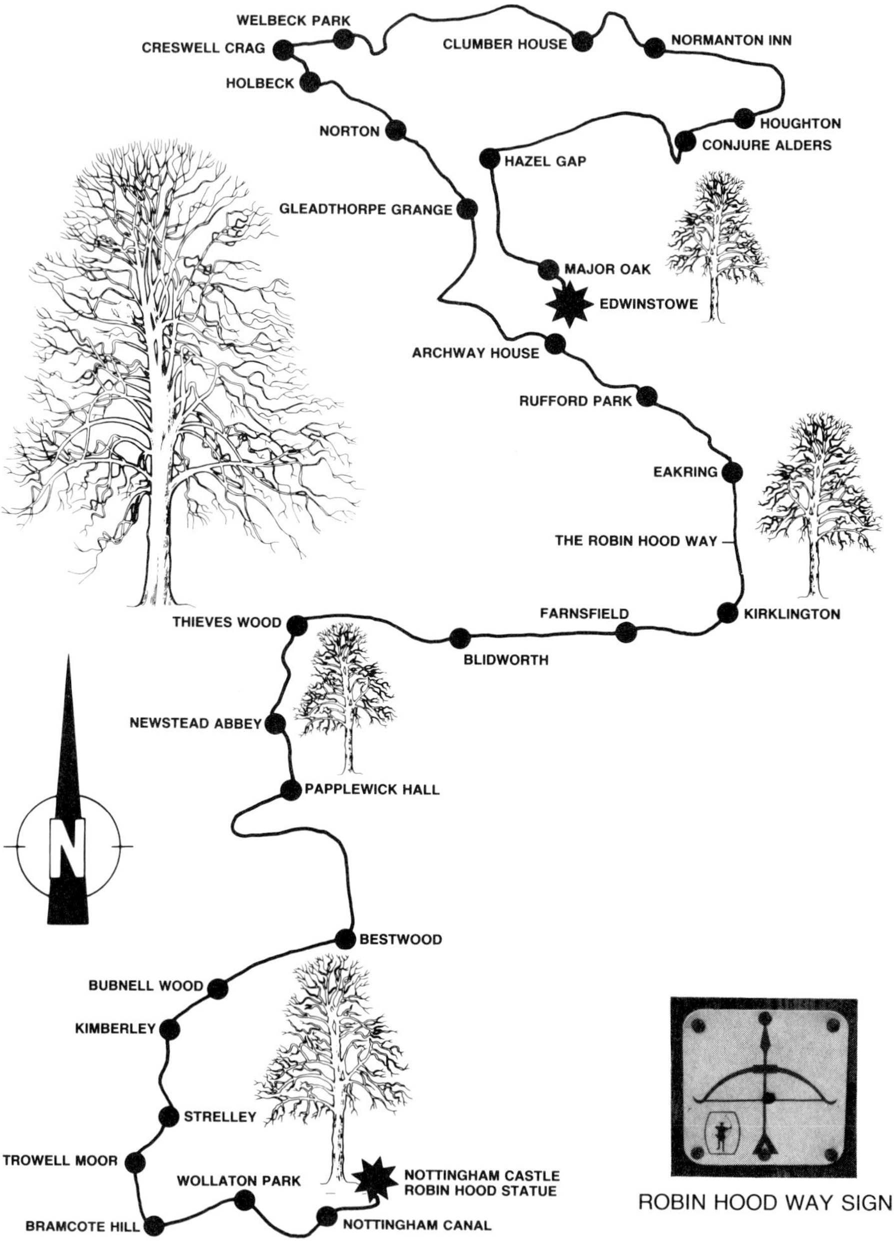

ROBIN HOOD WAY SIGN

THE ROBIN HOOD WAY — 88 MILES

Based on an idea by Christopher Thompson, the route was planned by members of the Nottingham Wayfarers's Rambling Club in commemoration of its Golden Jubilee year in 1982.

The walk is not circular but starts from Nottingham Castle in the south and weaves its way northwards to end at Edwinstowe. On the way the route passes through considerable woodland of Sherwood Forest and many places associated with Robin Hood. The region is relatively flat but as one would expect from a legendary area to be full of insterest encompassing a wide spectrum of attractions such as Major Oak, Creswell Crags, the Nottingham Canal, and impressive buildings such as Wollaton Hall and Rufford Abbey. The whole route is well signed with square discs displating a bow and arrow. The walk makes an ideal leisurely week's walk exploring the area and learning its secrets. Ammenities such as campsites and bed and breakfast are scarce, except at Edwinstowe. Towns just off the route such as Mansfield, Nottingham and Southwell have all the facilities. There are more than thirty inns on or close to the route and a few do bed & breakfast.

ROUTE OUTLINE —

Nottingham Castle — Nottingham Canal — Wollaton Park — Bramcote Hills — Trowell Moor — Strelley — Kimberley — Bulwell Wood — Bulwell Hall — Bestwood — Violet Hill — Papplewick Moor — Stoker Hill Farm — Burntstump Park — Papplewick Pumping Station — Blidworth Bottoms — Blidworth — Papplewick Hall — Newstead Abbey — Normanshill Wood — Thieves Wood — Harlow Wood — Providence Farm — Blidworth — Hill House Farm — Farnsfield — Southwell Trail — Kirklington — Roe Wood — Dilliner Wood — Eakring — Rufford Country Park — Holly Farm — Archway House — St Edwin's Chapel — Hanger Hill — Gleadthorpe Grange — Hazel Gap — Bentinck Lodge — Norton Village — Holbeck — Creswell Crags — Welbeck Park — South Lodge — Duchess Plantation — Clumber House — Hardwick — Normanton Inn — Pepperly Hill — Haughton — Conjure Alders — Spittalmoor — Freeboard Lane — Charcoal Plantation — Hazel Gap — Budby South Forest — Birklands — Major Oak — Edwinstowe.

MAPS —

O.S. 1:50,000 Sheet No 129 — Nottingham & Loughborough
O.S. 1:50,000 Sheet No 120 — Mansfield, Worksop & surrounding area
O.S. 1:25,000 Sheet No SK 43/53 — Nottingham (South West)
O.S. 1:25,000 Sheet No SK 44/54 — Nottingham (North)
O.S. 1:25,000 Sheet No SK 45/55 — Sutton in Ashfield
O.S. 1:25,000 Sheet No SK 46/56 — Mansfield (North)
O.S. 1:25,000 Sheet No SK 47/57 — Worksop (South) & Staveley
O.S. 1:25,000 Sheet No SK 65/75 — Southwell & Newark on Trent
O.S. 1:25,000 Sheet No SK 66/76 — Ollerton
O.S. 1:25,000 Sheet No SK 67/77 — Clumber Park & East Markham

GUIDEBOOK —

The Robin Hood Way Nottingham Wayfarers Rambling Club 1985

ROBIN HOOD

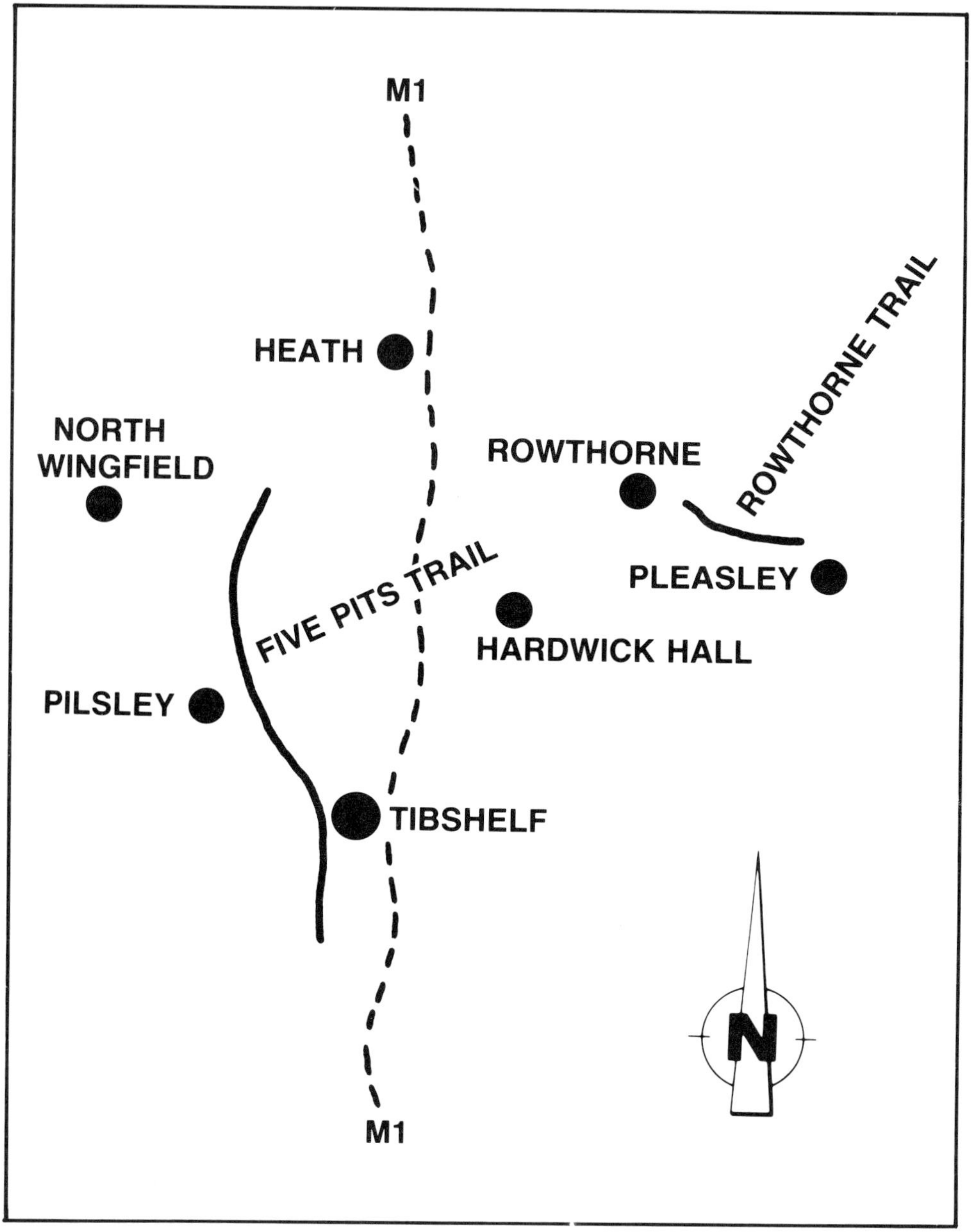
M1
HEATH
NORTH WINGFIELD
ROWTHORNE
ROWTHORNE TRAIL
PLEASLEY
FIVE PITS TRAIL
HARDWICK HALL
PILSLEY
TIBSHELF
N
M1

FIVE PITS TRAIL — 3½ MILES

The trail basically follows the line of the former Great Central Railway—part of the LNER and a major transporter of coal. The trail currently runs from Tibshelf in the south to Holmewood in the north, but as the name suggests it will eventually link the five Derbyshire collieries of Tibshelf, Pilsley, Holmewood, Williamthorpe and Grassmoor together. At Grassmoor a country park is being developed and the trail will end here. The colliery areas have been landscaped and forested and now provide a haven for wildlife. Car parks exist at Pilsley and near Tibshelf.

ROWTHORNE TRAIL — 1 MILE

A short walk along the line of the former Rowthorne/Glapwell Junction line to Hardwick Hall. The line closed in 1938 and passes through a particularly attractive wooded area east of Hardwick Park and makes an enjoyable bird spotting area.

Both trails are managed by the Derbyshire County Council and their Ranger Service.

MAPS -

- O.S. 1:25,000 Pathfinder Series Sheets Nos. SK46/56 and SK45/55

HARDWICK HALL

BOLSOVER DISTRICT WALK

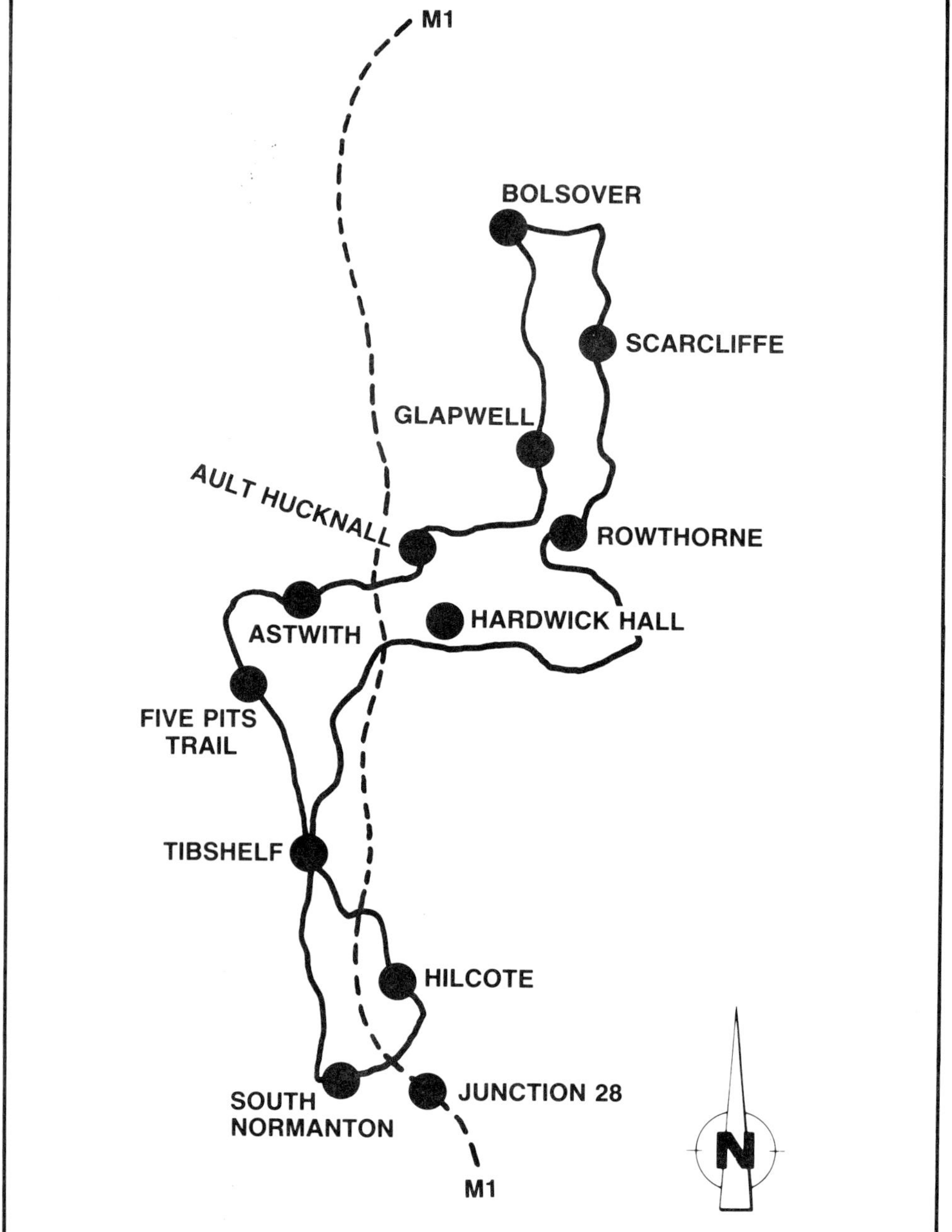

BOLSOVER DISTRICT WALK — 1985 ROUTE — 32 MILES

THE BOLSOVER DISTRICT WALK

Held annually on the Sunday of August Bank Holiday is a major walk for all to enjoy. Three separate distances and routes are walked in the Bolsover area — 6 miles (10km); 15 miles (25km); and 32 miles (52km). The walk was first held in 1982 and has become a major fixture of the U.K. Medal walks/marches of the Great Britain Federation of Popular Sports. Since its humble beginnings more than 2,000 people take part and together have raised more than £33,000 for Multiple Sclerosis Research. Like most of the walks in this book there is no time limit - it is simply a matter of walking round AND enjoying yourself. Being an organised event there is plenty of support and medals and a lot of memories of your walk around this area of Derbyshire. Cups are awarded to a wide ranging number of catorgries including, Largest Pub Team, Largest family, and a Vetrans Trophy. The winner of the latter in 1985 was Charlie Ellis, 85 years young!

The walk starts and ends at the South Normanton Community Centre, Mansfield Road, South Normanton. Camping is available here on the event weekend and accomodation is available locally. A very good and informative video of the 1984 is available on free loan. On Bank Holiday Monday following the walk the annual "Blister Ball" is held! The success of the walk has led to the formation of the South Normanton Walking Club and they have also organised an annual walk — the "Old Year'Obble" — held at the end of the year and again used to raise money for charity. The 1986 took place on 28th December and started/finished at the Pinxton Miners Welfare and was 6 miles (10km) long.

The Walk Director and further information can be obtained from –

Terry Whetton,
1, The Grange,
Broadmeadows,
South Normanton,
Derbyshire.
DE55 3ND

BOLSOVER CASTLE, THE TERRACE

DERBYSHIRE SIGN

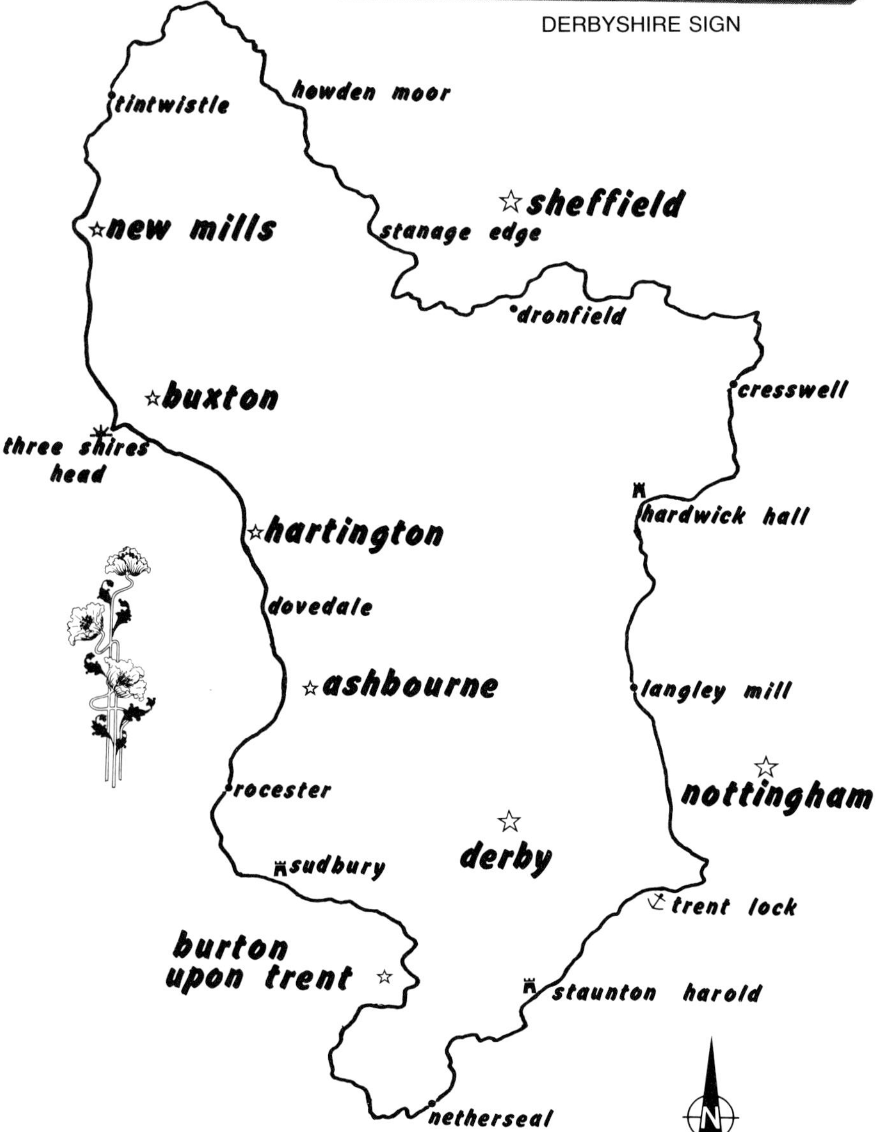

DERBYSHIRE BOUNDARY WALK — 280 Miles - Circular

During July 1977, I walked around the entire Derbyshire boundary. There is a footpath on or very close to the boundary. On paper, the overall mileage is 236 miles, but in reality the route is about 280. On the walk you see the whole spectrum of the Derbyshire landscape - Limestone dales, gritstone edges, gritstone moorland, industrial areas, canal walking and gentle rolling countryside. Added to this, you come to many of the fascinating historical buildings of the area, such as Sudbury Hall and Hardwick Hall.

If you have a couple of weeks to spare, I am sure you would find this walk very rewarding, and it will give you greater insight into Derbyshire. There is no guidebook to the walk- but I am writing one! My walk was linked to the National Trust, and it was for this reason that I set off from Sudbury Hall. Walking clockwise, I reached Sudbury Hall again 10½ days later. Being circular, you can of course start anywhere. Below is a breakdown of the route I took, with the relevant map numbers.

DAY	MAP O.S. 1:50,000	ROUTE	MILEAGE	OVERALL MILEAGE
1.	128 119	Sudbury Hall - Oaks Green - Palmer Moor - Doveridge - Dover Bridge - Eatonhall Farm - Rocester - Norbury - Church Mayfield - Mayfield - Mapleton - River Dove - Coldwell Bridge - Ilam.	20	20
2.	119	Ilam - Dovedale - Milldale - Wolfscote Dale - Beresford Dale - Hartington - Pilsbury - Crowdecote - Hollinsclough - Brand Top - Drystone Edge - Three Shires Head.	22	42
3.	119	Three Shires Head - Cheeks Hill - Can Holes - Buxton - Burbage - Wild Moor - Pym Chair - Kettleshulme - Handley Fold Farm - Bow Stones - Lyme Hall.	20	62
4.	110	Lyme Hall - Disley - New Mills - Mellor Moor - Robin's Hood Picking Rods - Chisworth - Charlesworth - Broadbottom - River Ethrow - Woolley Bridge - Tintwistle - Featherbed Moss - Howles Head - Round Hill - Black Hill - Holme Moss T.V.S. - Britland Edge Hill - Withins Edge.	24	86
5.	110 119	Withins Edge - Trigg - 499M - Salters Brook Bridge - Featherbed Moss - Howden Moors - Outer Edge - Margery Hill - Abbey Brook - Back Tor - Derwent Edge - Moscar Lodge - Stanage Edge - Burbage Valley - Longshaw.	24	110
6.	119 120	Longshaw - Whitemoor - Ramsley Moor - Grange Hill - Cutthorpe - Chesterfield - Barlow - Dronfield.	20	130

DAY	MAP O.S. 1:50,000	ROUTE	MILEAGE	OVERALL MILEAGE
7.	119 120	Dronfield - Troway - Ford - Eckington - Killamarsh - Whitwell - Steetley Chapel - Darfoulds - Hall Leys - Cresswell Crags - Whaley Thorns - Langwith - Shirebrook - Pleasley Vale.	25	155
8.	120 129	Pleasley Vale - Pleasley - Newboundmill Farm - Hardwick Hall - Stanley - Huthwaite - River Erewash - Pinxton - Pye Bridge - Ironville - Codnor Park - Stonyford - Langley Mill - River Erewash - Erewash Canal - Trowell - Sandiacre.	25	180
9.	129 128	Sandiacre - Long Eaton - River Trent - Trentlock - Sawley Out - Shardby - Trent & Mersey Canal - Swarkestone - Swarkestone Bridge - Kings Newton - Melbourne.	21	201
10.	128	Melbourne - Melbourne Parks - Scotland - Staunton Harold - Wickley Nook - Smisby - Ann Well Place - Blackfordby - Woodville - Moira - Hooborough Brook - Netherseal - River Mease - Clifton Campuille - Lullington - Coton on the Elms - Walton-on-Trent - River Trent - Burton-on-Trent.	23	224
11.	128	Burton-on-Trent - Rolleston on Dove - Tutbury - Scropton - Sudbury Hall.	12	236

MY SUPPORT VEHICLE

SUPPORT VEHICLE AND CEREMONIAL ARCH

SUDBURY HALL AND CAMP

CHESTERFIELD ROUND WALK — 45 MILES

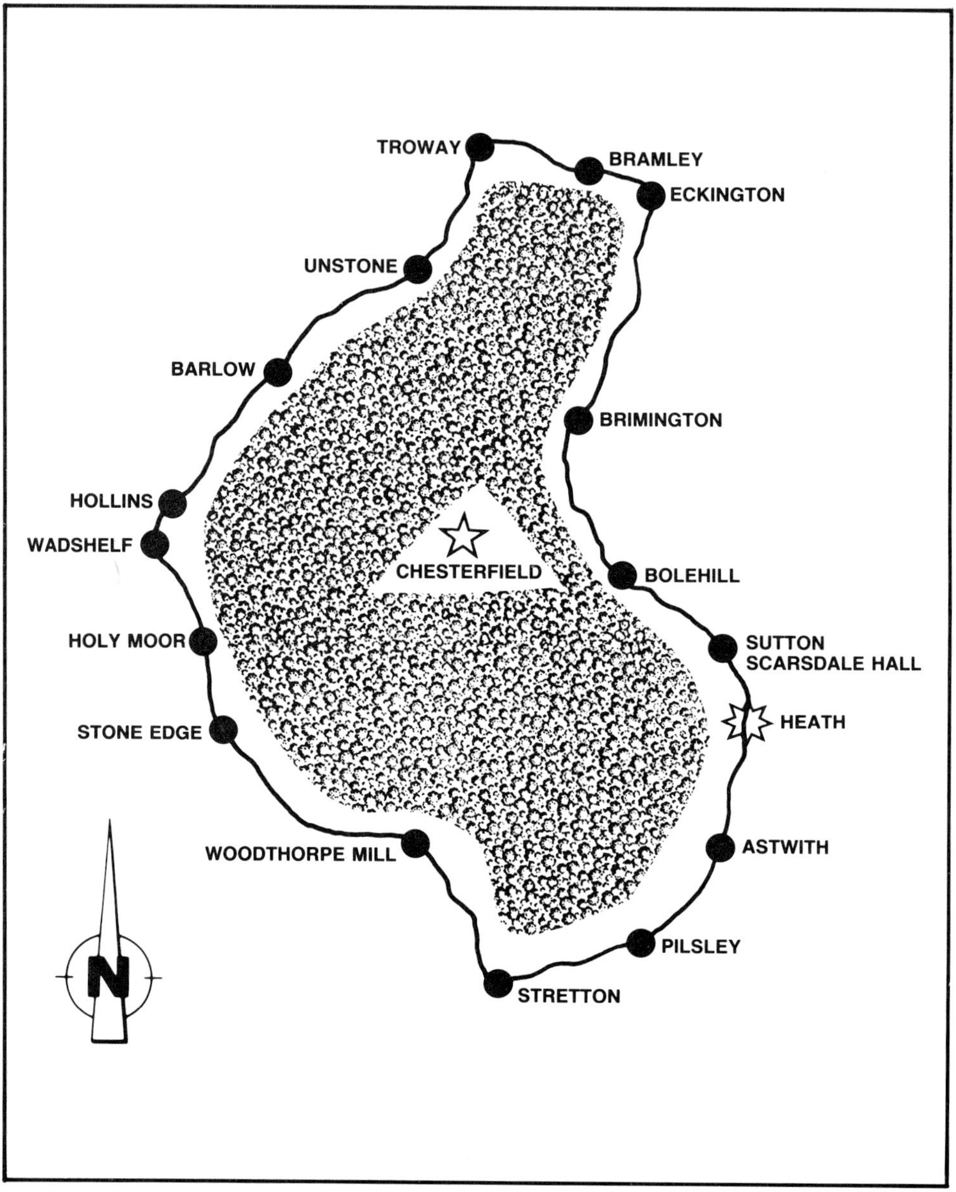

CHESTERFIELD ROUND WALK — 45 Miles

The walk was launched in 1985 by the members of the Chesterfield Town Group of the Ramblers' Association as part of the National Association's Golden Jubilee. The walk passes through unspoilt and attractive rolling countryside which is often overlooked by the serious walker who heads into the Peak District. Anyone who walks this route will be pleasantly surprised at its character and the many interesting villages en route. Being circular you can start it anywhere and you can walk it in stages getting transport back to central Chesterfield very easily. A recommended starting point is Heath to the east of the town and very accessible just off the M1 motorway.

ROUTE — (anti-clockwise direction) —

Heath — Astwith — Hardstoft — Pilsley — Stretton — Oxclose Farm — Newmarket — Woodthorpe Mill — Bole Hill Farm — Birkinlane Farm — Stone Edge — Holy Moor — Wadshelf — Hollins — Birley — Oxton Rake — Newgate — Barlow — Monk Wood — Unstone — Troway — Bramley — Eckington — White Lodge — South View Farm — Parkhouse Farm — Brimington — Brimington Common — Bole Hill — Rock Farm — Sutton Scarsdale Hall — Heath.

MAPS —

O.S. 1:50,000 Sheet No 119 — Buxton, Matlock and Dove Dale
O.S. 1:50,000 Sheet No 120 — Mansfield, Worksop & surrounding area
O.S. 1:25,000 Sheet No SK 27/37 — Chesterfield & Stoney Middleton
O.S. 1:25,000 Sheet No SK 47/57 — Worksop (South) & Stavely
O.S. 1:25,000 Sheet No SK 26/36 — Bakewell & Matlock
O.S. 1:25,000 Sheet No SK 46/56 — Mansfield (North)

GUIDEBOOK —

Chesterfield Round Walk by The Chesterfield Town Group of the Ramblers Association. Three sheets detail the following stages —

Heath to Stone Edge
Stone Edge to Troway
Troway to Heath.

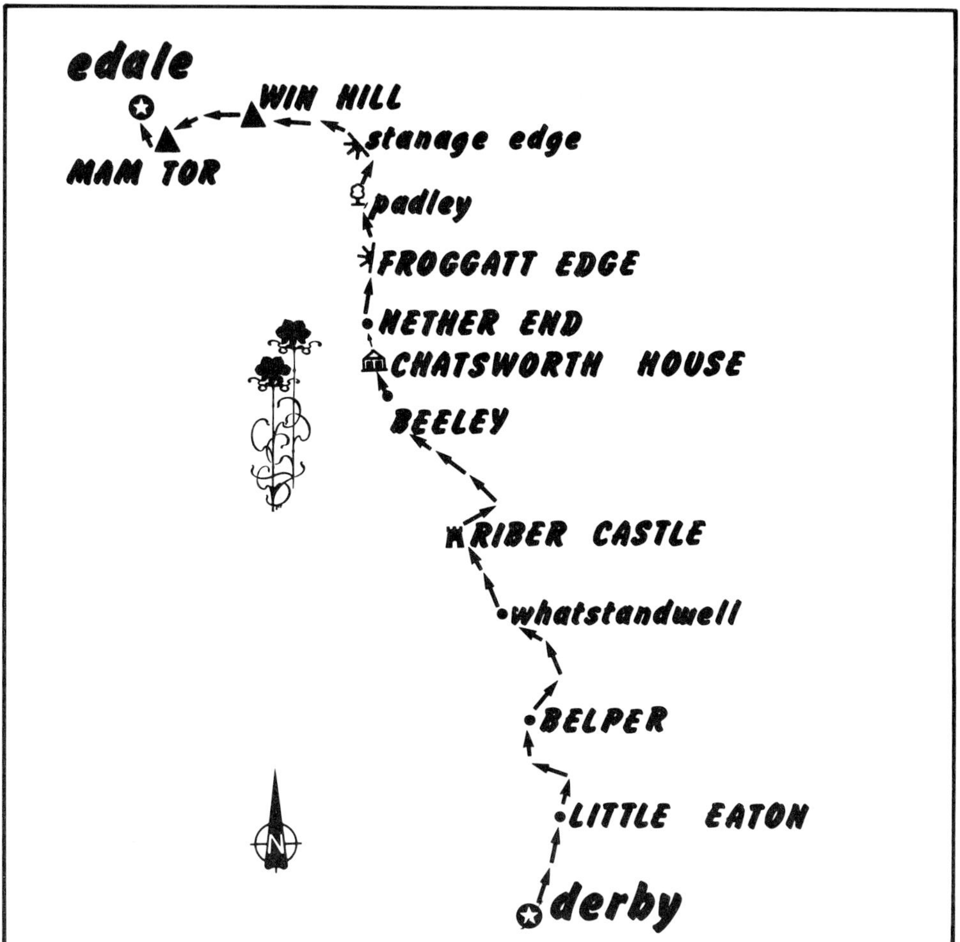

MAM TOR FROM CASTLETON

THE DERBYSHIRE GRITSTONE WAY — 56 Miles

Derby to Edale

Formulated by members of the Derbyshire Area Ramblers' Association in 1970.

Starting from the capital city of Derbyshire, the route takes you through the gritstone country to Edale, the start of the Pennine Way. At first the route lies through towns full of industrial archaeology with mills and water power; powered by the mighty river Derwent. Approaching the National Park boundary, the way becomes more "hilly" - to Riber Castle, Chatsworth, the gritstone edges, Lose Hill and finally Mam Tor. You can do the walk in as long or as short a time as you like - a weekend walk or a comfortable three days. It could be used as an extension to the Pennine Way.

ROUTE OUTLINE
Derby - Breadsall - Little Eaton - Holbrook - Milford - Belper - Nether Heage - Whatstandwell - Lea Bridge - Riber Castle - Tansley - Sycamore Farm - Beeley - Chatsworth Park - Baslow - Baslow Edge - Curbar Edge - Froggatt Edge - Padley Gorge - Burbage Edge - Stanage Edge - Win Hill - Lose Hill - Mam Tor - Edale.

MAPS
1:50,000 O.S. Sheet Nos. 128 - Derby and Burton-upon-Trent.
119 - Buxton, Matlock and Dovedale.
110 - Sheffield and Huddersfield.
1:25,000 O.S. Outdoor Leisure Map - The White Peak - central half.

GUIDEBOOK
The Derbyshire Gritstone Way by S. Burton, M. Maughan and I. Quarrinton. Thornhill Press 1980.

BADGE
Either by walking in one long walk, or in several different outings.
From: Max Maughan, 146 Vicarage Road, Mickleover, Derby.

ACCOMMODATION
Camp Sites - Whatstandwell, Matlock Moor, Baslow, Edale.
Youth Hostels - Ambergate, Matlock Bath, Bakewell, Eyam, Hathersage, Castleton, Edale.
Bed and Breakfast - Derby, Matlock, Rowsley, Baslow, Hathersage, Edale.

RIVER DERWENT AND BELPER MILL

THE DERWENT WATERSHED WALK — 40 MILES

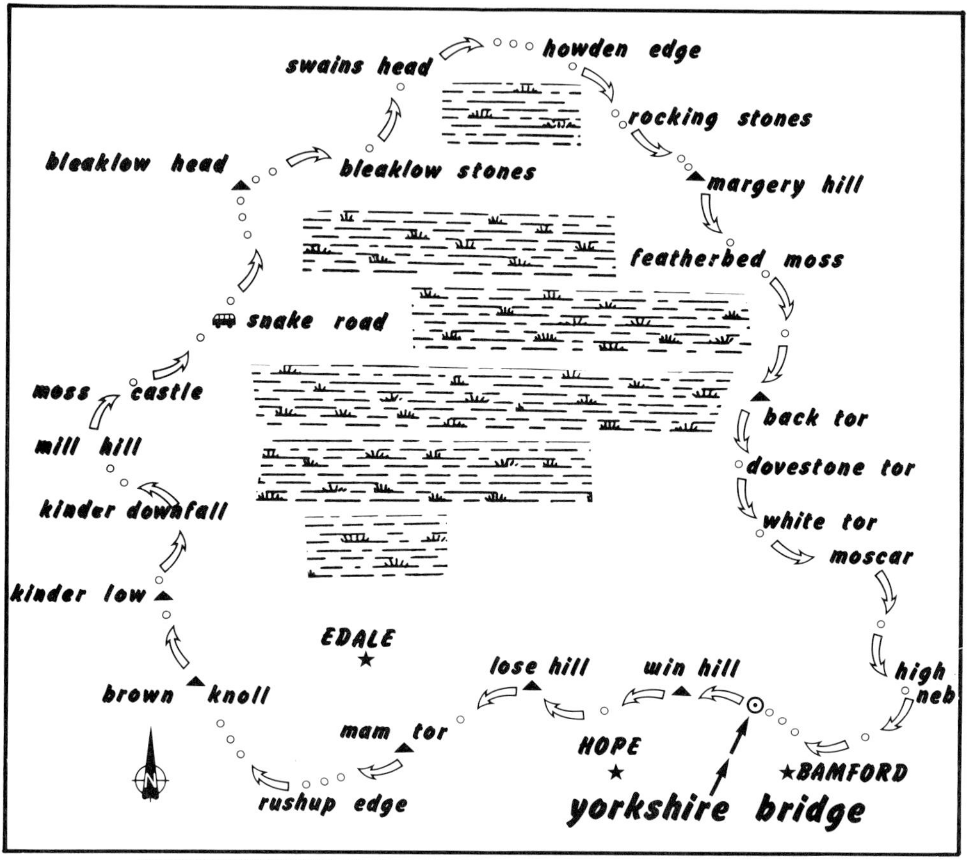

KINDER DOWNFALL, IN SUMMER

THE DERWENT WATERSHED WALK — 40 Miles Circular

First completed in 1918 by a party led by Eustace Thomas in 11 hours 39 minutes.

The toughest walk in the Peak District, across some of the hardest peat moorland to be found anywhere. It is not a route to be taken lightly, for to complete in a day - about 15 hours' walking - demands considerable stamina and determination. The walk can be split in two where the route crosses the Snake Pass; almost the halfway point. Once you have crossed this road you begin the toughest section across Bleaklow, with little chance of escape. Skill with a map and compass is essential, even during a summer's day, for the moorland is often featureless. There is considerable ascending and descending to do, which will tax your muscles to the limit. Despite all this it is a really magnificent challenge. Choose a summer day with long daylight hours so that you have plenty of time from dawn to dusk to complete the circuit at a pleasant steady pace.

ROUTE OUTLINE

Yorkshire Bridge (Bamford) - Win Hill - Lose Hill - Mam Tor - Rushup Edge - Brown Knoll - Kinder Downfall - Mill Hill - Moss Castle - Snake Road - Bleaklow Stones - Swains Head - Howden Edge - Rocking Stones - Margery Hill - Featherbed Moss - Back Tor - Dovestone Tor - Moscar - High Neb - Bamford Edge - Yorkshire Bridge.

MAPS

1:50,000 O.S. Sheet No. 110 - Sheffield and Huddersfield - whole route.
1:25,000 O.S. Outdoor Leisure Map - The Dark Peak - whole route except Stanage area.

GUIDEBOOKS

Walks in the Dark Peak by John N. Merrill. Dalesman 1982.
The Big Walks by K. Wilson and R. Gilbert. Diadem 1980.

ACCOMODATION

Close to route -
Campsites - Edale, Hope.
Youth Hostels - Castleton, Edale, Hagg Farm, Langsett.
Bed and Breakfast - Hope, Castleton and Edale.

VIEW FROM WIN HILL - DERWENT EDGE IN BACKGROUND

FOUR INNS WALK — 40 MILES

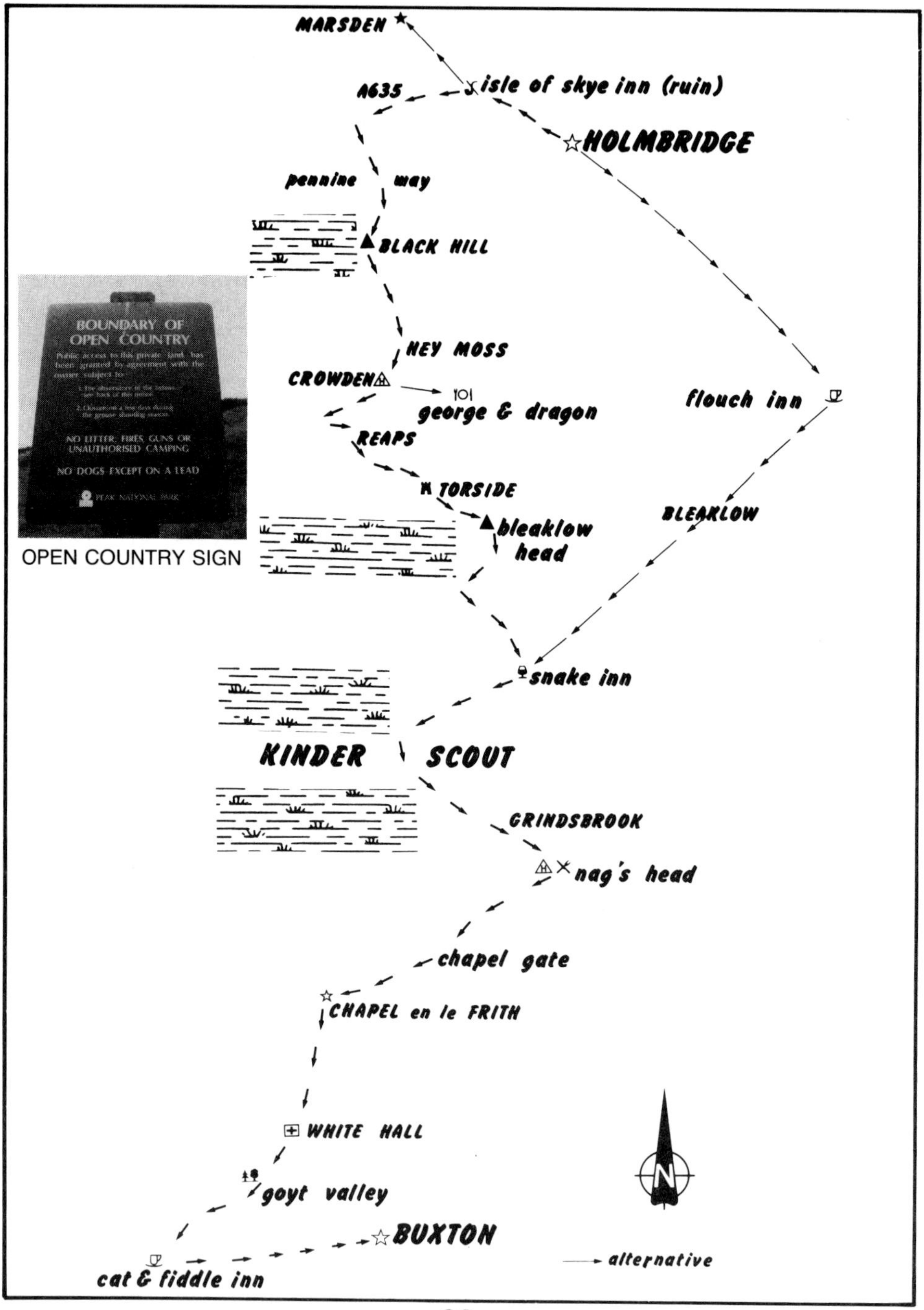

OPEN COUNTRY SIGN

FOUR INNS WALK - 40 Miles

Began as the Three Inns - 40 miles - inaugurated in 1922 - by F. Heardman, D. Berwick and H. E. Wild.

Route—Whaley Bridge - Cat & Fiddle - Kinder Scout - Snake Inn - Bleaklow - Black Hill - Isle of Skye Inn - Marsden.

Has now been extended to Four Inns - Isle of Skye (Ruins), Snake Inn, Nag's Head and Cat and Fiddle.

Some walkers have increased it to Five or more to include the George & Dragon at Woodhead, and the Flouch at Hazlehead. From 1957 it has become an annual Scout competition walk, with teams from all over the country competing for the fastest times, and trophies such as The Innsman, The Four Inns Cup and the Derbyshire Plate. More than 200 take part, with the first team completing the walk in about 9 hours.

The walk is another really excellent crossing of the high moorland plateaux of the High Peak.

ROUTE OUTLINE
Holmbridge Parish Hall - Site of Isle of Skye Inn - Hey Moss - Crowden - Reaps-Torside - Doctor's Gate - Snake Inn - Kinder Scout - Nags Head - Chapel-en-le-Frith - White Hall Outdoor Pursuits Centre - Cat & Fiddle Inn - Harpur Hill, Buxton.

MAPS
1:50,000 O.S. Sheet Nos. 110 - Sheffield & Huddersfield. 119 - Buxton, Matlock & Dovedale.
1:25,000 O.S. Outdoor Leisure Map - The Dark Peak.

ACCOMODATION
Camp Sites - Crowden and Edale.
Youth Hostels - Marsden, Crowden, Edale and Buxton.
Bed and Breakfast - Marsden, Edale and Buxton.

SNAKE INN SIGN

CAT & FIDDLE INN

MARSDEN TO EDALE — 25 MILES

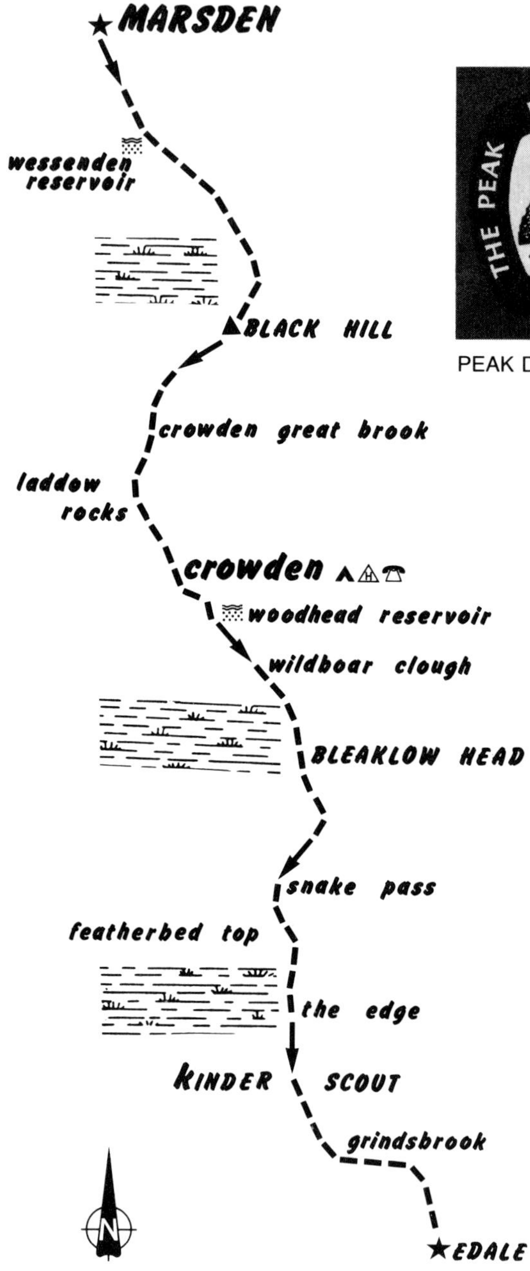

PEAK DISTRICT NATIONAL PARK SIGN

MARSDEN TO EDALE — 25 Miles

First completed by Ross Evans - date unknown.

The 'classic' walk of the High Peak, which has been walked since early this century and now forms the southern end of the Pennine Way. This is the tough section of the Pennine Way, over the peat moorlands masses of Black Hill, Bleaklow and Kinder. Whilst the Way takes a more weaving course, the Marsden to Edale route is more direct with steeper ascents.

The route has attracted many records - in the 1920's Fred Heardman did the first double crossing; in 1953 this was completed in under 13 hours. In December 1980 Rob Pearson ran it in 2 hrs. 39 minutes; you should allow about 10 hours! The person to have walked it most would appear to be Harry Buckley, for in September 1953 he made his 116th crossing. The route can be done from either direction, but the north to south way is the most popular - it is all downhill! Crowden can be used as the half-way point, making the walk an enjoyable weekend crossing.

ROUTE OUTLINE
Marsden - Wessenden Reservoir - Wessenden Head - Pennine Way - Black Hill - Crowden Great Brook - Laddow Rocks - Crowden - Wildboar Clough - Bleaklow Head - Devil's Dyke - Snake Road (A57) - Featherbed Top - Ashop Clough shooting cabin (ruins) - The Edge - Kinder Scout - Grindsbrook - Edale.

MAPS
1:50,000 O.S. Sheet No. 110 - Sheffield and Huddersfield - whole route.
1:25,000 O.S. Outdoor Leisure Map - The Dark Peak - section from Wessenden Head Moor to Edale.

GUIDEBOOKS
Walks in the Dark Peak by John N. Merrill. Dalesman 1982.
The Big Walks by K. Wilson and R. Gilbert. Diadem 1980.

ACCOMODATION
Camp Sites - Crowden and Edale.
Youth Hostels - Marsden, Crowden and Edale.
Bed and Breakfast - Marsden and Edale.

GRINDSBROOK

THE MASTER'S HIKE — 45 MILES

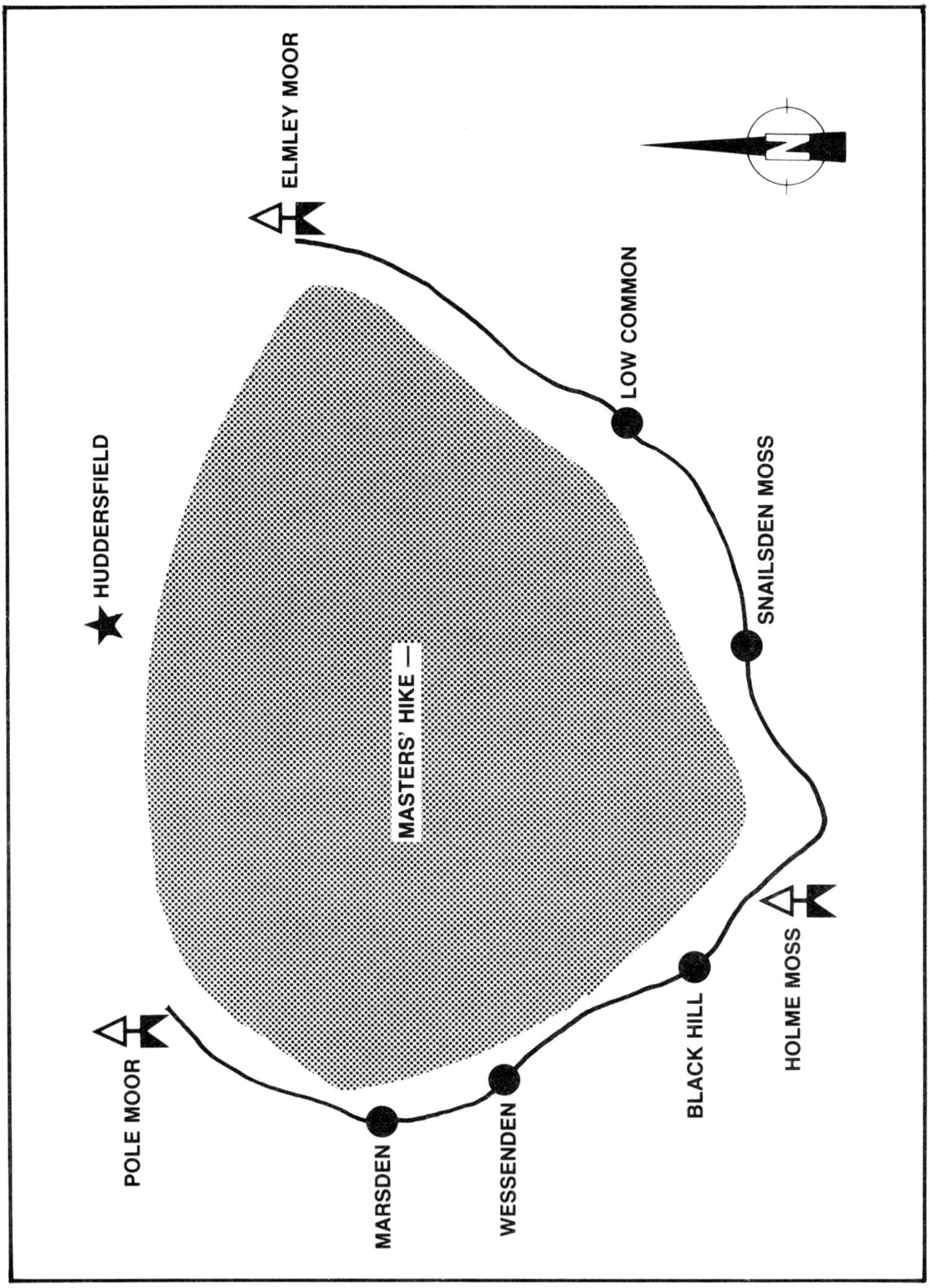

THE MASTER'S HIKE — 45 MILES

Like the Four Inns Walk this is an annual walking event organised by the Scouts, and in 1985 by the Holme Valley Scouts. The walk begins from Huddersfield and as the name implies takes in the three TV masts at Pole Moor, Holme Moss and Emley. Lying on the northern end of the Peak District National Park and mostly rugged and bleak moorland, the walk is a strenuous but rewarding challenge and makes an ideal summer route making your own route between the masts. In 1985 the fastest lady around the route was Alison Wright in 10 hours 26 minutes. A very good time when you consider that the Peak Ventures fourth team took 19½ hours!

MAPS —

O.S. 1:50,000 Sheet No 110 — Sheffield and Huddersfield
O.S. 1:25,000 Outdoor Leisure Map — The Dark Peak

MAP READING ON BLEAKLOW

LADDOW ROCKS

CIRCULAR WALKS AROUND KINDER AND BLEAKLOW

The following four walks are not challenge walks but ones to enjoy encircling the principal areas of the Dark Peak. All are covered on the O.S. 1:25,000 Outdoor Leisure Map — The Dark Peak, and have been detailed in my books — Long Circular Walks in the Peak District and Walks in the Dark Peak. All are tough walks involving considerable ascent and descent and at around 20 miles each make a good, hard but enjoyable day's walk. They are the grandslam of the moorland expanses of the Peak District and should not be taken light heartedly for they are serious undertakings where expertise with map and compass is necessary.

THE EDALE SKYLINE ROUTE — 20 MILES

ROUTE —

Cheshire Cheese Inn, Hope — Lose Hill — Back Tor — Mam Tor — Rushup Edge — Brown Knoll — Edale Cross — Nether Tor — Mad Woman Stones — Hope Cross — Win Hill — Cheshire Cheese Inn, Hope.

KINDER CIRCUIT — HIGH LEVEL ROUTE — 18 MILES

ROUTE —

Edale — Grindsbook — Crowden Tower — Pym Chair — Noe Stool — Edale Rocks — Kinder Low — Kinder Downfall — The Edge — Fairbrook Naze — Seal Edge — Seal Stones — Blackden Edge — Crookstone Knoll — Madwoman's Stones — Ringing Roger — Edale.

KINDER CIRCUIT — LOW LEVEL ROUTE — 24 MILES

ROUTE —

Edale — Ollerbrook Booth — Rowland Cote Youth Hostel — Jagger's Clough — Crookstone Barn — Blackley Clough — Alport Bridge — Hayridge Farm — Oyster Clough — Snake Inn — Ashop Clough — Ashop Head — William Clough — Kinder Reservoir — Kinder Bank Hayfield) — Coldwell Clough — Edale Cross — Jacob's Ladder — Upper Booth — Edale.

AROUND BLEAKLOW — 20 MILES

ROUTE —

Birchin Clough — Over Wood Moss — Alport Low — Pennine Way — Bleaklow Head — Bleaklow Hill — Bleaklow Stones — Grinah Stones — Barrow Stones — River Derwent — Slippery Stones — Howden Reservoir — Ditch Clough Plantation — Alport Castles — Alport Castles Farm — Hayridge Farm — Course of Roman Road — Birchin Clough.

MAP —

O.S. Outdoor Leisure Map — The Dark Peak

KINDER'S THREE WISE MEN

EDALE CROSS

THE RAMBLERS'WAY — 38 MILES

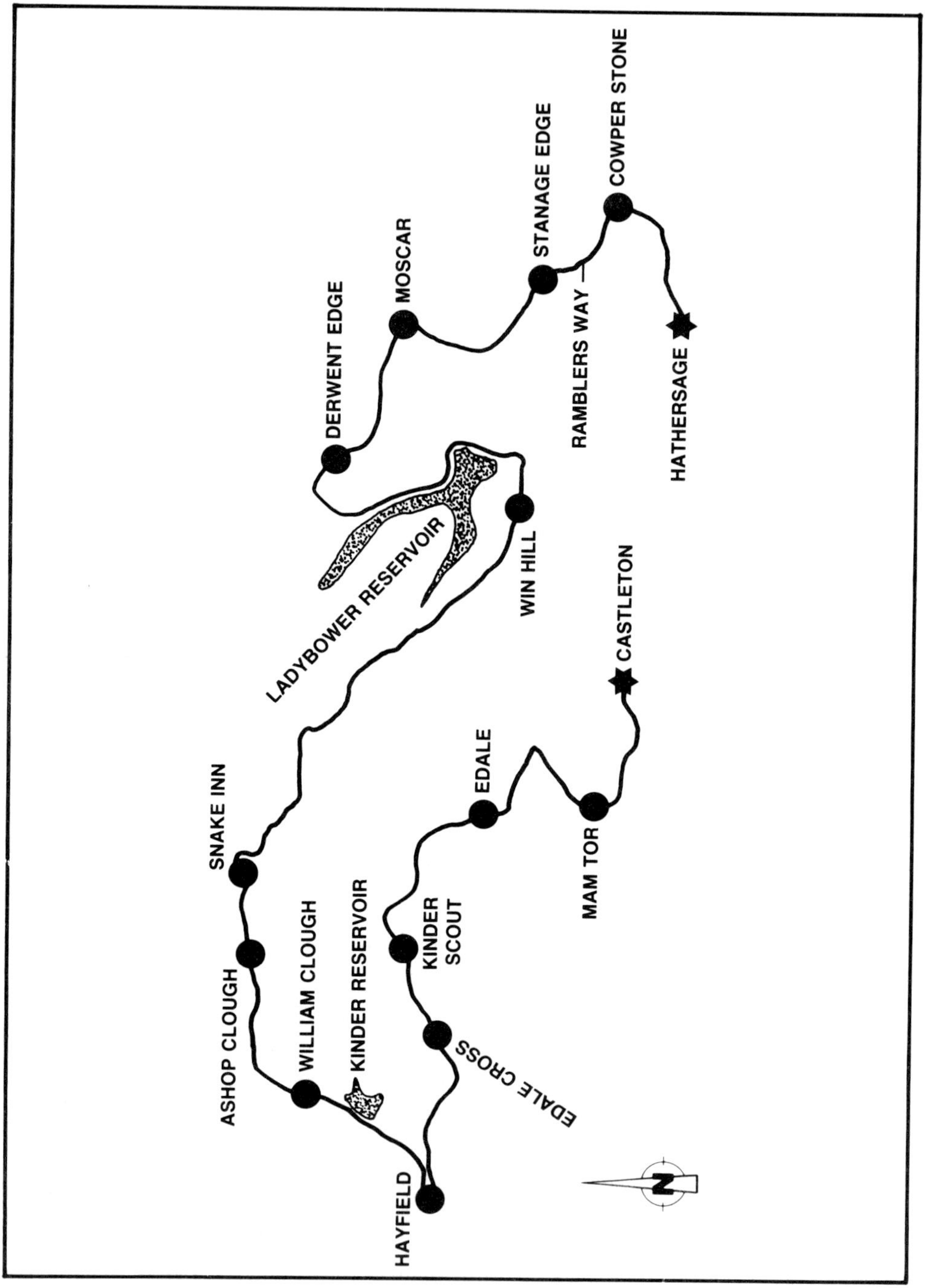

THE RAMBLERS WAY — 38 MILES

First walked by Andrew Newton and Paul Summers in June 1983

Whilst being an interesting and a demanding day challenge walk over the gritstone country of the Peak District, it can be walked as a two day walk or even in stages. The walks basic theme, as the name implies, is to the Ramblers who struggled before the advent of National Parks for the freedom of the hills. The walk traces the route of the Great Trespass of 1932 and a chapter in the guidebook to the walk details the history and fight for the Open Country.

ROUTE OUTLINE –

Castleton — Mam Tor — Edale — Grindslow Knoll — Hayfield — Kinder Reservoir, William Clough — Snake Path — Snake Inn — Hayridge Farm — Wooler Knoll — Win Hill — Yorkshire Bridge — Derwent Edge — Crow Chin — High Neb — Stanage Edge — Cowper Stone — Hathersage.

The walk involves 5,300 feet of ascent and the highest point reached is Grindslow Knoll — 2,000 feet.

MAPS –

O.S. 1:50,000 Sheet No 110 — Sheffield and Huddersfield
O.S. 1:25,000 Outdoor Leisure map — The Dark Peak

GUIDEBOOK –

The Ramblers Way by Andrew Newton and Paul Summers 1983

BADGES –

From 'Mountain Peaks Climbing Club', 17 Humberston Road, Wollaton, Nottingham. NG8 2SU.

ACCOMODATION — on or close to the route

Bed & Breakfast — Castleton, Edale, Hayfield, and Hathersage
Youth Hostels — Castleton, Edale, Hathersage and Hagg Farm.
Camping Sites — Castleton, Edale, Hayfield, Hagg Farm, Hathersage.
Inns — 19 along the route with the aptly named Ramblers Inn in Edale.

THE RAMBLER INN, EDALE

THE LIMEY WAY, Derbyshire Peak District

A 40 MILE WALK THROUGH 18 LIMESTONE DALES. CREATED BY JOHN N. MERRILL ON AN INAUGURAL WALK IN 1969

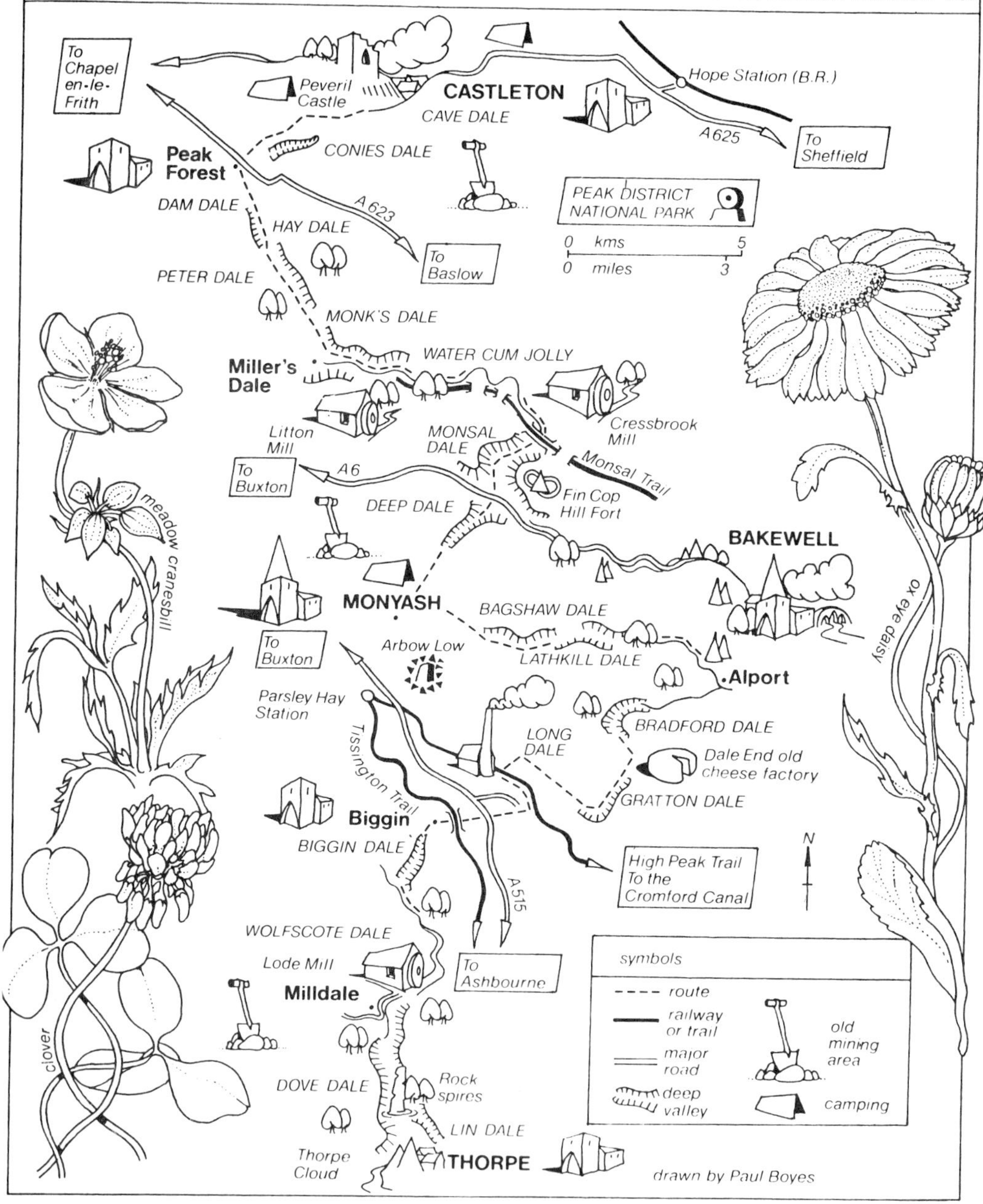

THE LIMEY WAY - 40 Miles

Castleton to Thorpe via 18 limestone dales

Devised and inaugurated by John N. Merrill in June 1969.

I first did this walk in 1969, and gave it scant mention in my book - Peak District Walks 2 — Long Walks for the Rambler. It was not until six years later that rights of way were made through some of the dales, making it possible to include further limestone dales. The aim of the walk is to walk through as many limestone dales as possible from the most northern end of the limestone area to its southern end. Some of the dales are popular - this is unavoidable - but much of the route is through very quiet and beautiful limestone scenery. My guidebook to the route came out in 1979, and so far more than 2,000 people have successfully completed it in either 24 or 48 hours. One enterprising person walked it twice over the weekend - to Thorpe on the Saturday and back to Castleton on the Sunday! The average walking time is between 10 and 14 hours, with many people using Monyash or Youlgreave YHA, where there is a register, as the halfway point.

ROUTE OUTLINE

Castleton (Market Place) - Cave Dale - Old Moor - Peak Forest - Dam Dale - Hay Dale - Peter Dale - Monk's Dale - Miller's Dale - Water cum Jolly - Monsal Dale - Deep Dale - Monyash - Bagshaw Dale - Lathkill Dale - Alport - Bradford Dale - Dale End - Gratton Dale - Long Dale - High Peak Trail - Biggin - Biggin Dale - Wolfscote Dale - Milldale - Dovedale - Lin Dale - Thorpe.

MAPS

1" O.S. Tourist Map - The Peak District - whole route.
1:50,000 O.S. Sheet Nos. 110 Sheffield & Huddersfield. 119 Buxton, Matlock & Dovedale.
1:25,000 O.S. Outdoor Leisure Map - The White Peak.

GUIDEBOOK —

Full details from John N. Merrill at JNM Publications

BADGES AND COMPLETION CERTIFICATES —

Two colour embroidered badges with signed certificate from JNM Publications.
Red cloth badge — for crossing made within 24 hours
Green cloth badge — for crossing made within 48 hours.

ACCOMODATION

On or close to route.
Camp Sites - Castleton, Rowter Farm, Haddon Grove, Thorpe.
Youth Hostels - Castleton, Miller's Dale, Bakewell, Youlgreave, Hartington and Ilam.
Bed and Breakfast - Castleton, Peak Forest, Monsal Dale, Monyash, Hartington, Ashbourne.

There are a dozen inns on or close to the route!

Since 1969 more than 50,000 people have successfully completed the walk and raised more than £100,000 for charity.

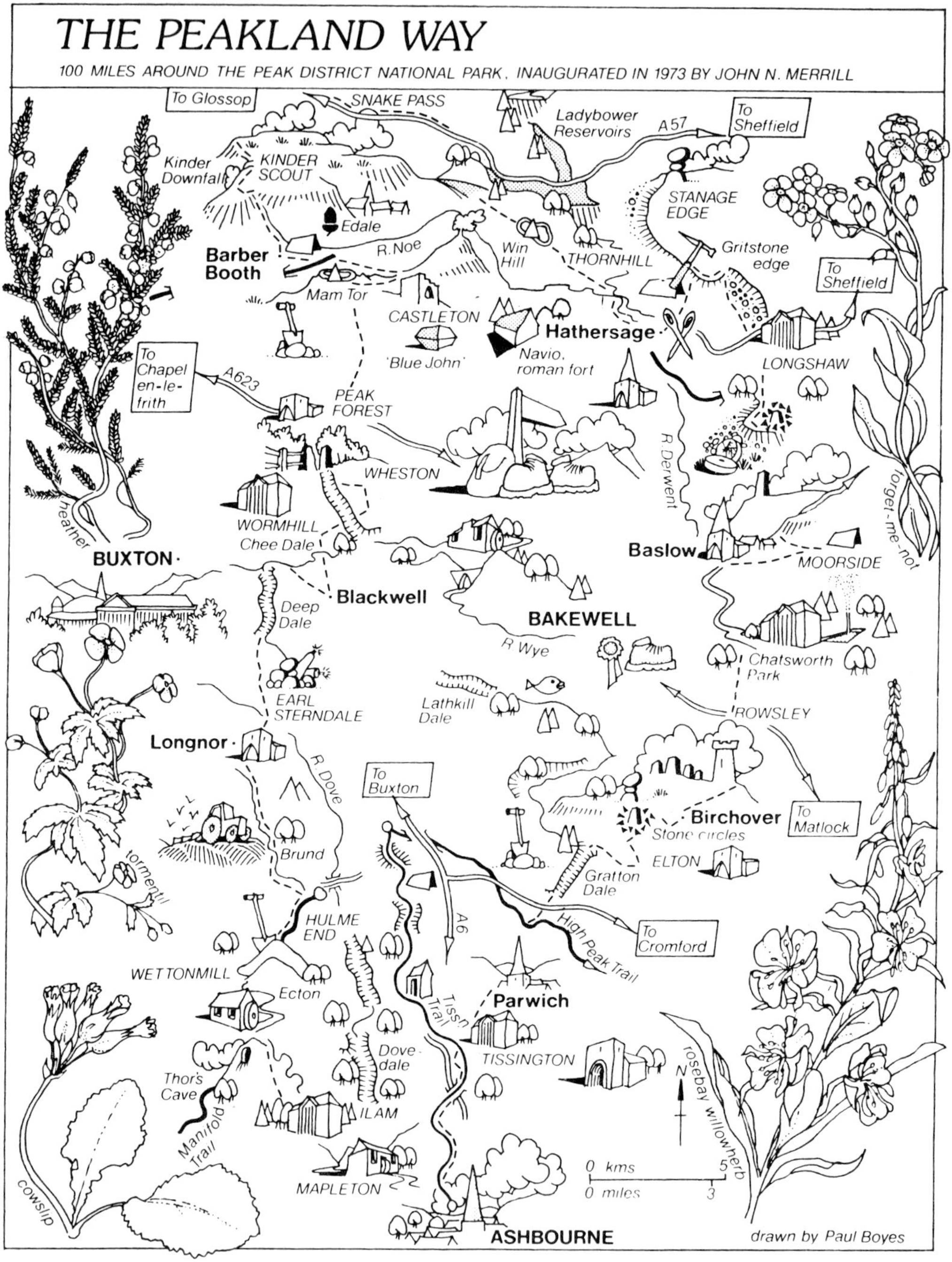
THE PEAKLAND WAY
100 MILES AROUND THE PEAK DISTRICT NATIONAL PARK, INAUGURATED IN 1973 BY JOHN N. MERRILL
To Glossop
SNAKE PASS
Ladybower Reservoirs
A57
To Sheffield
Kinder Downfall
KINDER SCOUT
STANAGE EDGE
Edale
R.Noe
Win Hill
THORNHILL
Gritstone edge
Barber Booth
Mam Tor
To Sheffield
CASTLETON
Hathersage
'Blue John'
Navio, roman fort
LONGSHAW
To Chapel en-le-frith
A623
PEAK FOREST
R.Derwent
WHESTON
WORMHILL
Chee Dale
Baslow
MOORSIDE
BUXTON
Blackwell
Deep Dale
BAKEWELL
R.Wye
Chatsworth Park
EARL STERNDALE
Lathkill Dale
ROWSLEY
Longnor
R.Dove
To Buxton
Birchover
To Matlock
Stone circles
Brund
ELTON
Gratton Dale
HULME END
A6
High Peak Trail
To Cromford
WETTONMILL
Parwich
Ecton
Tissington Trail
Dove-dale
TISSINGTON
Thor's Cave
ILAM
N
Manifold Trail
0 kms 5
0 miles 3
MAPLETON
ASHBOURNE
drawn by Paul Boyes
heather
forget-me-not
tormentil
rosebay willowherb
cowslip

THE PEAKLAND WAY - 100 Miles - Circular

Around the Peak District National Park, from Ashbourne.

Devised and inaugurated by John Merrill in August 1973.

I had felt for a long time that the Peak District lacked its own long distance footpath. I decided to remedy the situation. My criteria for the walk was to encompass as much of the scenic variety of the area as possible - limestone dales, gritstone edges and gritstone moorland. Wherever I could, I selected paths that were little used, but on the edges and moorland there is no option but to use the popular ones. The walk can be backpacked, hostelled or bed and breakfast, and can be completed in eight easy stages - a week's walk. The more determined can do it in four days. Badges are available for those who have successfully walked it, and a Peakland Way Club for Peakland Wayers, with an annual weekend planned each December at a Peakland hotel for a meal, slide show and Sunday walk. More than 1,000 people have walked the route within the eight day period.

ROUTE OUTLINE

Stage One - 10 miles - Ashbourne - Mapleton - Littlepark - Coldwall Bridge - Ilam - Musden Grange - Throwley Hall - Beeston Tor - Weag's Bridge - Thor's Cave - Wettonmill.

Stage Two - 15 miles - Wettonmill - Ecton - Hulme End - Hulme House - Brund Mill - Pool - Over Boothlow - Longnor - Cave - Earl Sterndale - Brierlow Grange - Horseshoe Dale - Deep Dale - Chee Dale - Blackwell.

Stage Three - 13 miles - Blackwell - Chee Dale - Wormhill - Monksdale House - Wheston - Dale Head - Hay Dale - Dam Dale - Peak Forest - Broctor - Old Moor - Windy Knoll - Mam Tor - Hollins Cross - Barber Booth.

Stage Four - 13 miles - Barber Booth - Upper Booth - Jacob's Ladder - Kinder Low (2,077 ft.) - Kinder Downfall - Ashop Head - Snake Path - Snake Inn - Course of Roman Road - Hayridge Farm - Roman Road - Rowlee Bridge - Rowlee Farm - Hagg Farm.

Stage Five 11 miles - Hagg Farm - Hope Cross - Roman Road - Win Hill - Thornhill - Shatton - River Derwent - Hathersage.

Stage Six - 13 miles - Hathersage - Stanage Plantation - Stanage Edge - Cowper Stone - Burbage Rocks - Longshaw Lodge - Sheffield Plantation - Grouse Inn - Froggatt Edge - Curbar Edge - Baslow Edge - Wellington's Monument - Gardom's Edge - Moorside Farm.

Stage Seven - 11 miles - Moorside Farm - Baslow - Chatsworth Park - Beeley - Rowsley - Congreave - Stanton-in-Peak - Stanton Moor - Birchover.

Stage Eight - 15 miles - Birchover - Hermit's Cave - Elton - Oddo House Farm - Gratton Dale - Mouldridge Grange - High Peak Trail - Lowmoor Far m- Parwich - Tissington - Tissington Trail - Ashbourne.

MAPS
1" O.S. Tourist Map - The Peak District - whole route.
1:50,000 O.S. Sheet Nos. 110 - Sheffield & Huddersfield. 119 Buxton, Matlock & Dovedale.
1:25,000 O.S. Outdoor Leisure Map - The Dark Peak. The White Peak.

GUIDEBOOK —

Full details from John N. Merrill at JNM Publications.

BADGE AND COMPLETION CERTIFICATE —

Two colour embroidered badge on a blue cloth together with signed certificate from JNM Publications.

ACCOMODATION
On or close to the route.
Camp Sites - There is a camp site at each stage of the route.
Youth Hostels - Ilam Hall, Hartington, Buxton, Ravenstor, Castleton, Edale, Hagg Farm, Hathersage, Bakewell, Elton and Youlgreave.
Bed and Breakfast - Ashbourne, Longnor, Castleton, Edale, Hathersage, Baslow, Rowsley.

PEAKLAND WALKERS AT ASHBOURNE

KINDER DOWNFALL IN WINTER

THE RIVERS' WAY — 43 MILES

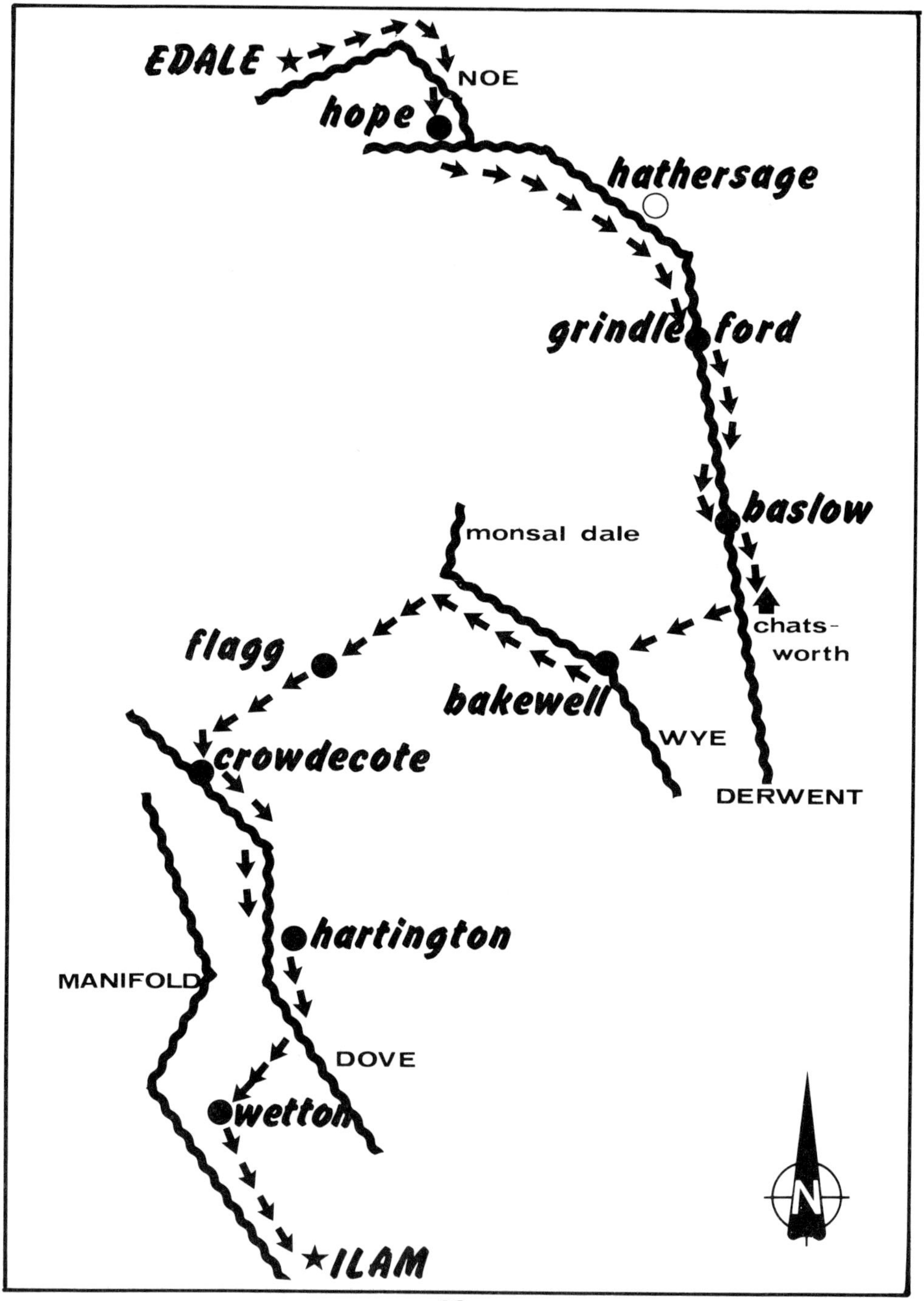

THE RIVERS' WAY - 43 Miles

From Edale to Ilam via river valleys.

Devised, created and inaugurated by John Merrill in August 1983.

Fourteen years have passed since I created the Limey Way. The other obvious walking route from north to south through the Peak District was via the main river systems. The route starts from the end of the Pennine Way at Edale and is a logical continuation of the walk from the hills to the plains. The route links together the five principal rivers of the Peak District - the Noe, Derwent, Wye, Dove and Manifold. It is a challenge to walk the way in a day - about 14 hours - but with Bakewell being half-way it can be done comfortably over two days or even four! The walk can also be a marathon pub crawl with more than twelve inns passed en route! For a really challenging 80 mile walk it is possible to start at Edale and walk the Rivers' Way the first day to Ilam and return to Castleton via the Limey Way the next day!

ROUTE OUTLINE
Edale - YHA - Jaggers Clough - River Noe - Hope - Navio - Shatton - River Derwent - Leadmill Bridge - Grindleford - Froggatt - Calver - Baslow - Chatsworth Park - Edensor - Ball Cross - Bakewell - River Wye - Ashford in the Water - Deep Dale - Flagg - Pomeroy - Alderly Cliff - River Dove - Crowdecote - Pilsbury - Hartington - Beresford Dale - Narrowdale - Wetton - River Manifold - Castern Hall - Ilam.

MAPS
O.S. 1:25,000 Outdoor Leisure Map - The Dark Peak
O.S. 1:25,000 Outdoor Leisure Map - The White Peak.
O.S. 1:50,000 Landranger series sheet No. 110 - Sheffield and Huddersfield.

GUIDEBOOK —

The Rivers' Way John N. Merrill JNM Publications 1986

BADGE AND COMPLETION CERTIFICATE —

A four colour embroidered badge on a blue cloth together with a signed certificate is available from JNM Publications

ACCOMODATION
On or close to the route.
Bed and Breakfast - Edale, Hathersage, Grindleford, Bakewell, Ashford in the Water, Crowdecote, Hartington, Wetton, Ilam.
Youth Hostels - Edale, Hathersage, Bakewell, Hartington, Ilam.
Camping Sites - Edale, Hope, Bakewell, Pomeroy, Wetton, Ilam.

BAKEWELL'S FIVE ARCHED BRIDGE OVER RIVER WYE

PEAKLAND HERITAGE WALK — 36 MILES

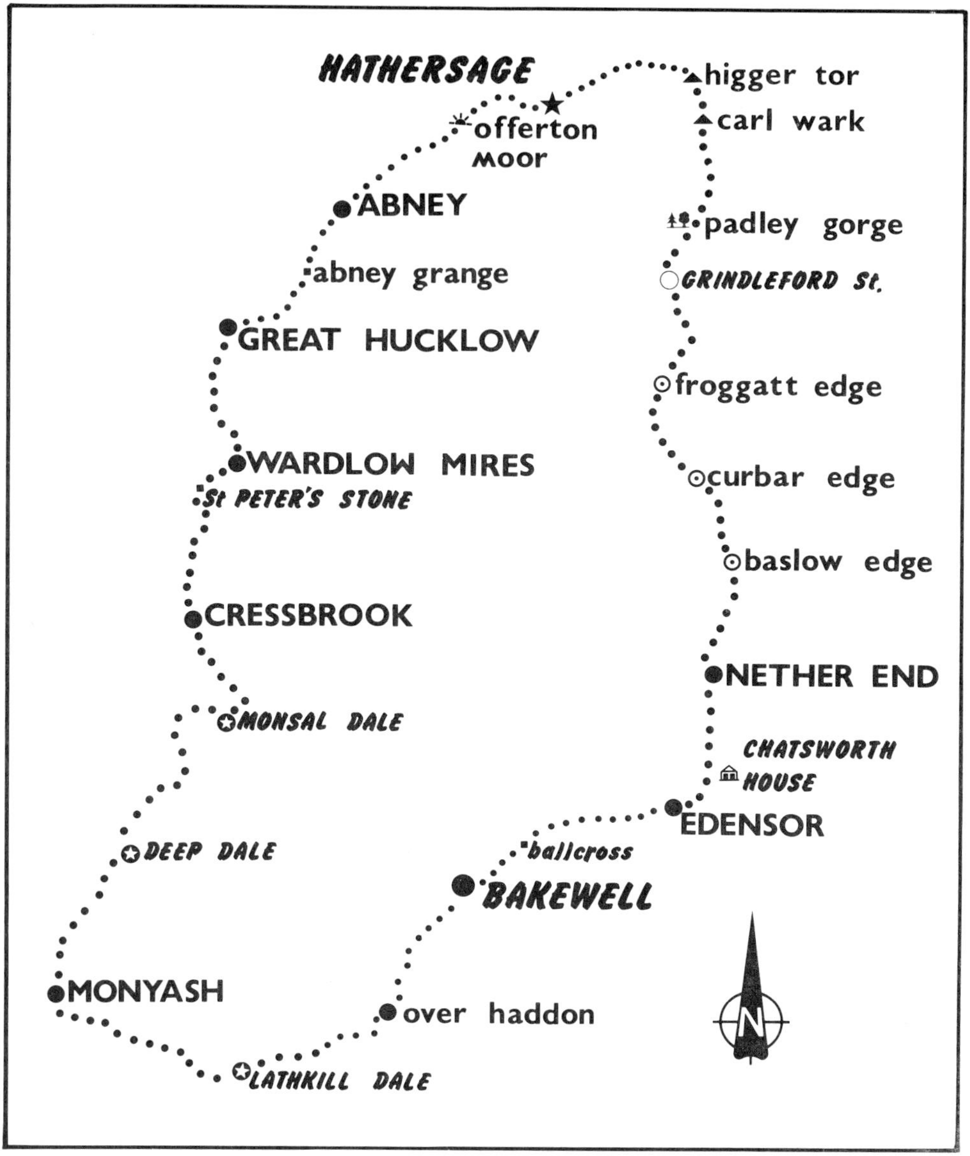

PEAKLAND HERITAGE WALK — 36 Miles

Circular walk around central Peakland

Devised by Tony Wimbush of the West Yorkshire Long Distance Walkers Association. A circular walk linking together many of the scenic gems of the central area of the Peak District. Much of the route includes sections of the Peakland Way and Limey Way, and does in fact join the two together. Can be completed in one day, but can be made into a pleasant two-day walk, using Bakewell or Hathersage as the half way point. The route goes anti-clockwise.

ROUTE OUTLINE

Hathersage - Offerton Moor - Abney - Great Hucklow - Wardlow - Peter's Stone - Ravensdale Cottages - Cressbrook - Monsal Dale - Deepdale - Monyash - Lathkill Dale - Over Haddon - Bakewell - Ballcross - Chatsworth - Netherend (Baslow) - Baslow Edge - Curbar Edge - Froggatt Edge - Grindleford Station - Padley Gorge - Carl Wark - Hathersage.

MAPS

1" Tourist Map - The Peak District - whole route.
1:50,000 O.S. Sheet Nos. 110 - Sheffield & Huddersfield. 119 - Buxton, Matlock & Dovedale.
1:25,000 O.S. Outdoor Leisure Map - The White Peak.
Leaflet - from Haritage Secretary - Mrs. M. Hickling, School House, Stocksbank Road, Mirfield, West Yorks.

BADGE & CERTIFICATE

From above address.
Red badge if completed under 15 hours.
Green badge if completed over 15 hours.

ACCOMMODATION

On or close to the route.
Camp Sites - Hathersage, Haddon Grove and Eric Byne Memorial Camp Site near Birchens Edge.
Youth Hostels - Hathersage, Ravenstor and Bakewell.
Bed and Breakfast - Hathersage, Monsal Head, Monyash, Over Haddon, Bakewell and Baslow.

CHATSWORTH HOUSE AND DERWENT

THE GRITSTONE EDGE WALK — 23 MILES

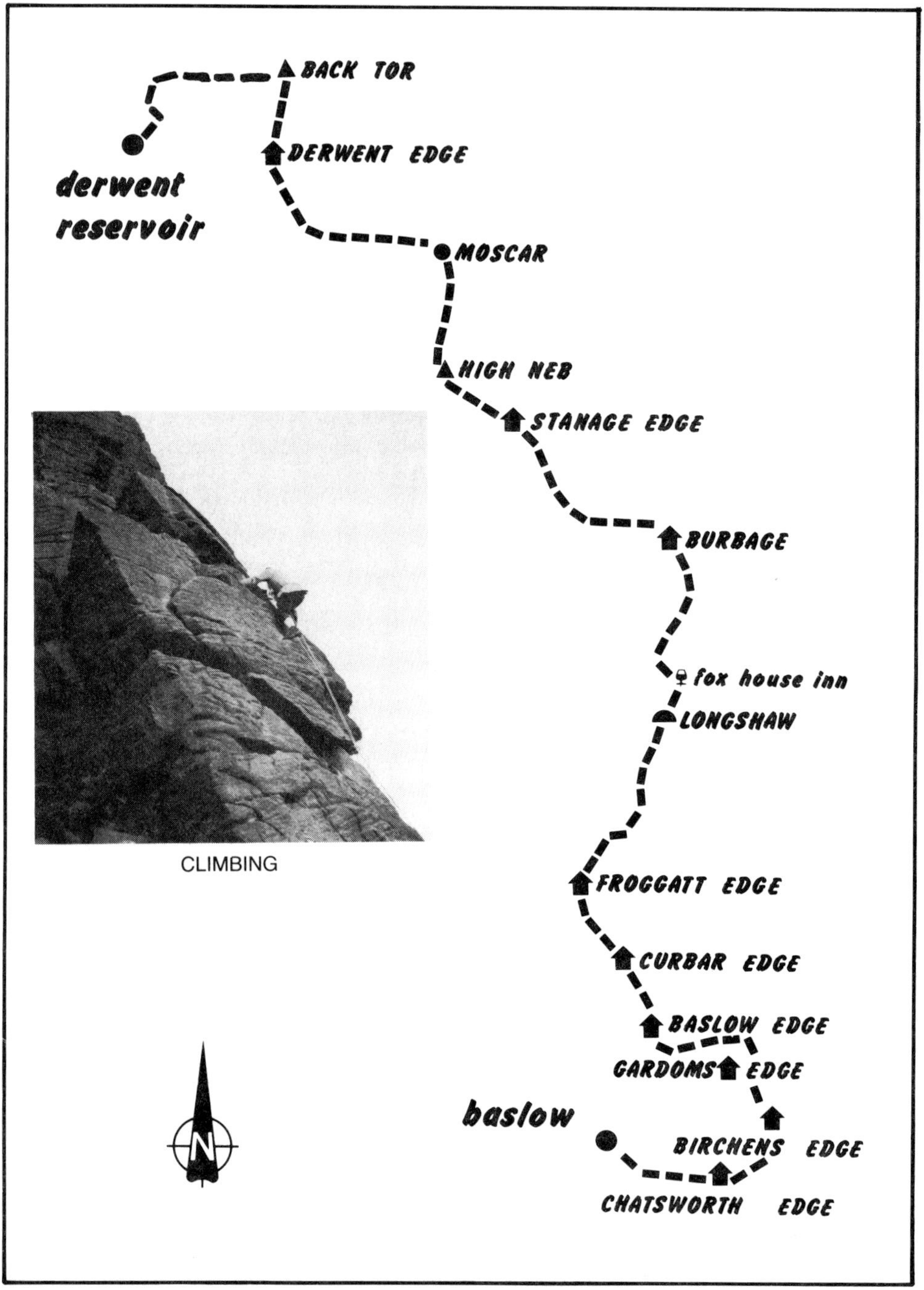

CLIMBING

THE GRITSTONE EDGE WALK — 23 Miles

I have done this walk more than forty times and the Limestone Dale walk over thirty times! I usually do the Gritstone Edge walk on New Years day, to recover from the previous night's festivities. My rules are simple; do a climb on every edge and have a drink on every edge. I set off with a bottle of whisky, a chicken leg and a hunk of Christmas cake. The climbs are hard at first but as the walk and alchohol take effect the easier they are! I reach Baslow foodless and bottleless!

The walk is devised to be done in a single day with your wife, girlfriend or support party dropping you off at Fairholmes car park. The first three miles are the hardest as you ascend to Back Tor. From there, as you head southwards you are basically heading downhill with a few brief ascents. There are virtually no amenities along the route, apart from two inns that you pass more than halfway along the route. Baslow, the end, has everything!

At the Burbage Valley with there being several paths you can select which one — either down the valley, along the top of the edge or over Higger Tor and Carl Wark. Upon reaching Wellington's Monument at the end of Baslow Edge, there is an easy way straight down to Baslow, but this is frowned upon as there are three more edges to go!

ROUTE OUTLINE —

Derwent Reservoir — Back Tor — Derwent Edge — Moscar — Stanage Edge — Burbage Edge — Longshaw — Froggatt Edge — Curbar Edge — Baslow Edge — Birchens Edge — Chatsworth Edge — Baslow.

MAPS —

O.S. 1:25,000 — Outdoor Leisure Map — The Dark Peak
O.S. 1:25,000 — Pathfinder Series — Sheet No SK28/38 — Sheffield
O.S. 1:25,000 — Outdoor Leisure Map — The White Peak — East Sheet

GUIDE BOOK —

Peak District End to End Walks John N. Merrill JNM Publications 1986

BADGES AND COMPLETION CERTIFICATES —

A four colour embroidered badge on a brown (Gritstone) backgound is available with certificate from JNM Publications.

ACCOMODATION —

Youth Hostel — Hagg Farm 1½ miles from start of route
Camping — Eric Byne Memorial Campsite, Birchen Edge
Bed & Breakfast — Baslow

THE LIMESTONE DALE WALK — 24 MILES

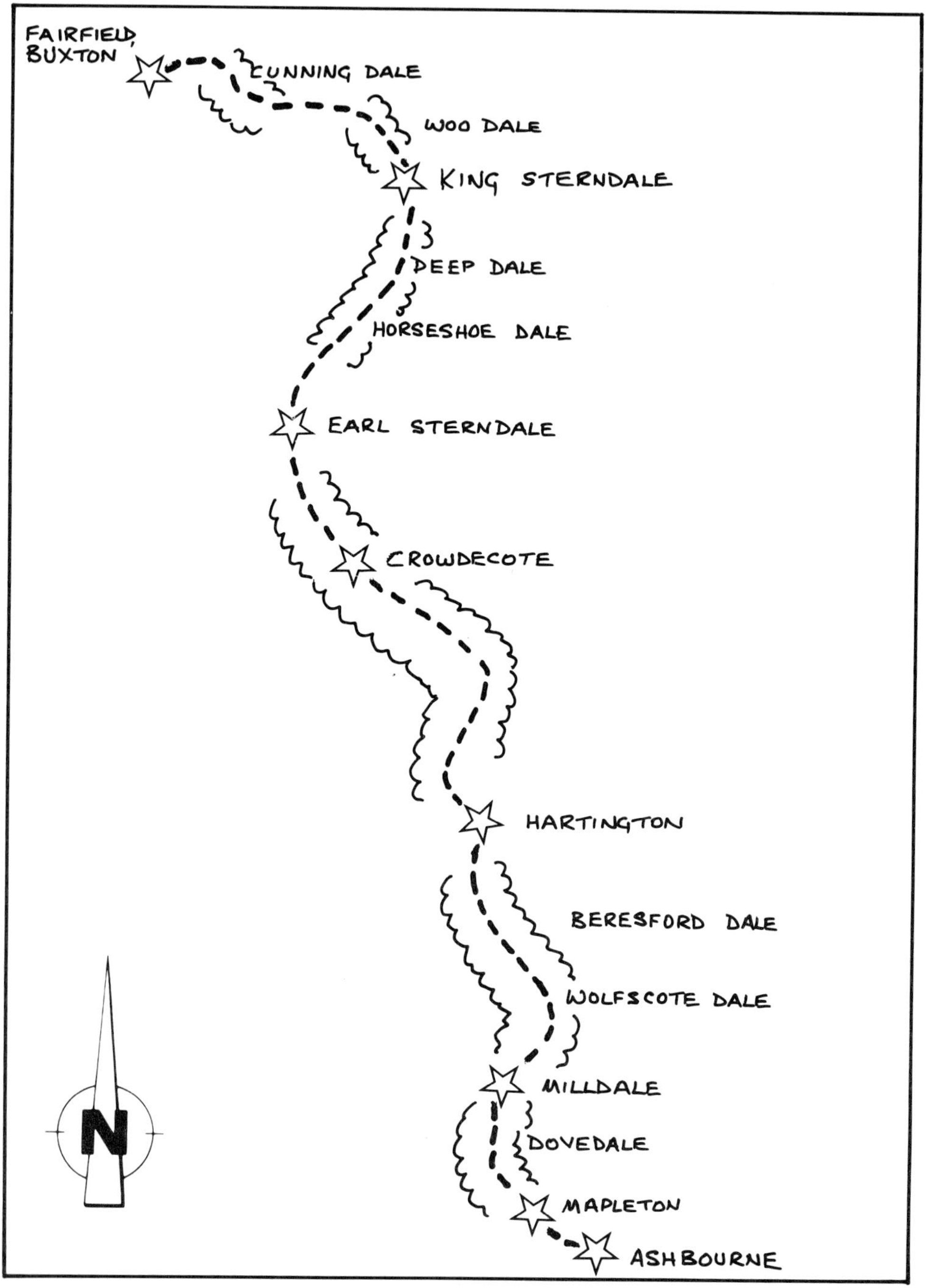

THE LIMESTONE DALE WALK — 24 Miles

Like the Gritstone Edge walk, this is another day job, with you being deposited at the start at Fairfield, on the outskirts of Buxton. Again it is a north to south route with only 1,400 feet of ascent on the way; much of the route is in the descent mode. Apart from a couple on inns, The Quiet Woman at Earl Sterndale and the Packhorse Inn at Crowdecote, there are no other facilities until Hartington, just over the halfway point. Up to here the walking has been through a variety of quiet dales with no one to be seen.

The section from Hartington to the end of Dovedale is popular, and best avoided on Sundays and Bank Holidays in the summer months. Beyond is again quiet and solitude until you gain the Market Place and Cross in Ashbourne, where full facilities are to hand.

ROUTE —

Fairfield, Buxton — Cunning Dale — Woo Dale — King Sterndale — Deep Dale — Horseshoe Dale — Earl Sterndale — Crowdecote — Hartington — Beresford Dale — Wolfscote Dale — Milldale — Dove Dale — Mapleton — Ashbourne.

MAPS —

O.S. 1:25,000 Outdoor Leisure Map — The White Peak — west sheet
O.S. 1:25,000 Pathfinder Series — Sheet No SK 04/14 — Ashbourne and the Churnet Valley.

GUIDEBOOK —

Peak District End to End Walks John N. Merrill JNM Publications 1986.

BADGES & COMPLETION CERTIFICATES

Four colour embroidered badge on a grey (limestone) background and certificate from JNM Publications.

ACCOMMODATION —

Bed and Breakfast — Buxton, Crowdecote, Hartington, Ashbourne
Youth Hostels — Buxton, Hartington, Ilam
Camping — Buxton, Hartington, Ashbourne

HORSESHOE DALE

JOHN MERRILL'S PEAK DISTRICT CHALLENGE WALK — 25 MILES

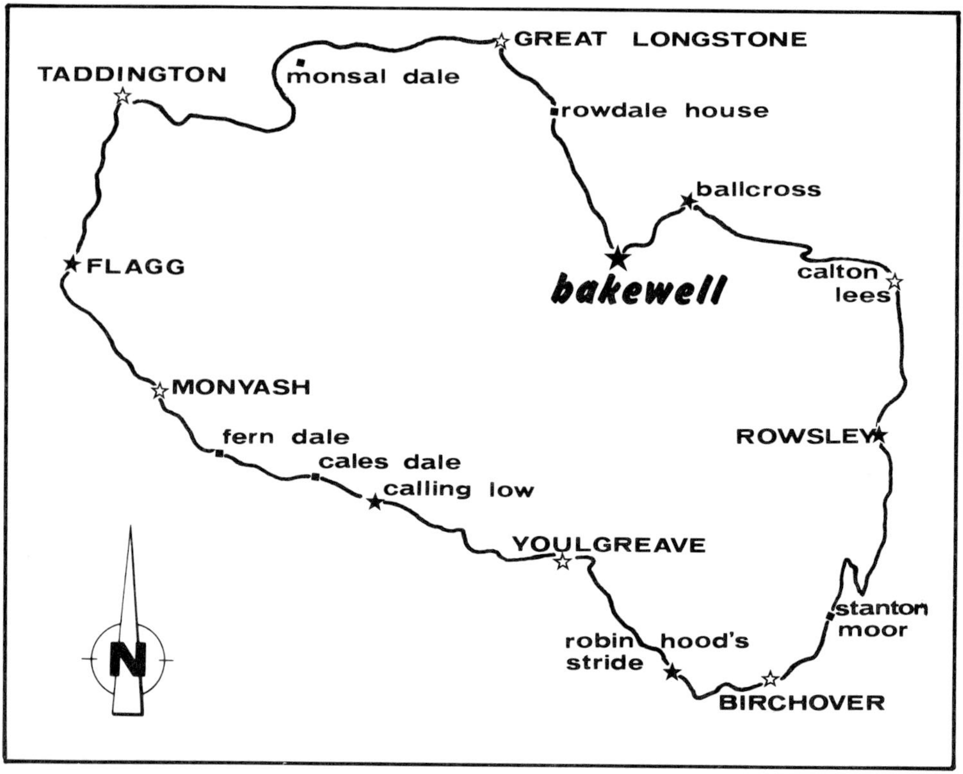

MONSAL DALE AND VIADUCT

JOHN MERRILL'S PEAK DISTRICT CHALLENGE WALK — 25 Miles — Circular

Around central area of the Peak District, from Bakewell.

Devised, created and inaugurated by John Merrill in December 1982.

The fine traditional market town of Bakewell is the central point of the Peak District, and a logical starting point for a challenge walk in the area. My aim has been to create —

1. a circular walk, using footpaths as much as possible
2. a walk that could be accomplished within a day — 10 hours
3. a challenge, making the route as rugged as possible, but one that is within everyone's capability.
4. to combine as much scenic variety in the route as possible

Bearing these points in mind, the walk takes you through the limestone scenery — plateaux and dales; across gritstone moorland and past rocky outcrops; and along river valleys. The paths are in the main little used ones. Several of the well-known areas such as Monsal Dale will be seen from different angles providing stunning views. En route are numerous historical sites and ancient monuments. You pass through several villages where there are shops and inns to 'help you' on your way.

By the end of 1986 more than 5,000 people have completed the walk in an average time of 10 hours. The longest on record is 16 hours, and the fastest — running — is 4hrs 14mins; this was their third attempt! Many have used the walk to raise money for charity, and so far approximately £55,000 has been raised.

ROUTE OUTLINE
Bakewell - Ballcross - Calton Lees - River Derwent - Rowsley - Stanton Woodhouse - Stanton Moor - Birchover - Robin Hood's Stride - Youlgreave - Calling Low - Cales Dale - Fern Dale - Monyash - Flagg - Taddington - Deep Dale - Brushfield House - Monsal Head - Great Longstone - Rowdale House - Bakewell.

MAPS
1:25,000 O.S. Outdoor Leisure Map - The White Peak
1:50,000 O.S. Sheet No. 119 - Buxton, Matlock and Dovedale.
— Both cover whole route.

GUIDEBOOK —

John Merrill's Peak District Challenge Walk John N. Merrill JNM Publications 1986

BADGES AND COMPLETION CERTIFICATES —

A four colour embroidered badge on a yellow cloth is available with certificate from JNM Publications. JNM Publications also maintain a register of all who complete this and other walks created by John N. Merrill.

ACCOMODATION
Youth Hostels - Bakewell, Youlgrave and Elton.
Bed & Breakfast - Bakewell, Monyash, and Monsal Head.
There are eight inns on the route!

THE MINERS WAY — 68 MILES

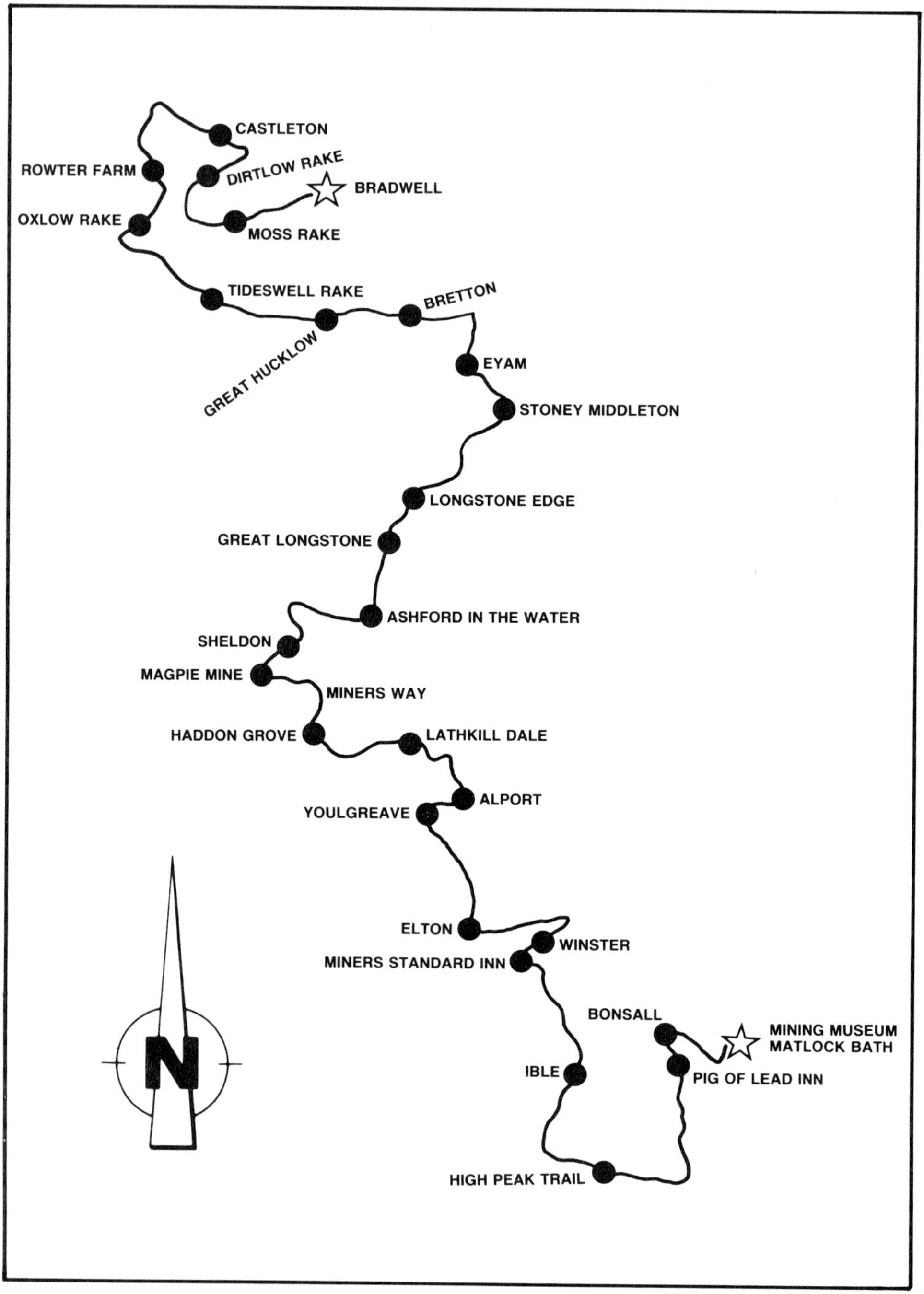

THE MINERS WAY — 68 MILES

Inaugurated in August 1983 to celebrate the 25th Anniversary of the Peak District Mines Historical Society Ltd.

A walk, as the name suggests, that links together many of the principal lead mining areas in the Peak District. Whilst the walk makes a very interesting walk through the limestone scenery of the Peak District it is very much a historical walk and is worth spending five or more days walking the route to appreciate and learn about the area. The walk begins at the Mining Museum in Matlock Bath and ends at Bradwell. It can backpacked or bed and breakfasted or completed in stages; their is no time limit.

ROUTE —

Matlock Bath — Bonsall — High Peak Trail — Griffe Grange Farm — Ible — Winster — Elton — Youlgreave — Lathkill Dale — Magpie Mine — Sheldon — Ashford — Great Longstone — Longstone Edge — Stoney Middleton — Eyam — Sir William Hill — Bretton — Great Hucklow — High Rake — Tideswell Rake — Oxlow Rake — Rowter Farm — Castleton — Dirtlow Rake — Moss Rake — Bradwell.

The route can be broken down into five stages —

Matlock Bath to Winster — 13 1/2 miles
Winster to Haddon Grove Farm — 14 miles
Haddon Grove Farm to Stoney Middleton — 15 1/2 miles
Stoney Middleton to Rowter Farm — 12 miles
Rowter Farm to Bradwell — 13 miles

MAPS –

O.S 1:25,000 Outdoor Leisure Map — The White Peak
O.S.1:25,000 Outdoor Leisure Map — The Dark Peak

GUIDEBOOK –

The Miners Way by A.Pearce, J. Watson and Rachel Watston 1983

BADGE AND GUIDEBOOK –

Can be obtained from — Miss R Watson, 138 Ladywood Road, Kirk Hallam, Ilkeston, Derbyshire.

ACCOMMODATION — on or close to the route

Camp Sites — Winster, Haddon Grove Farm, Eyam, Rowter Farm, Hope
Youth Hostels — Matlock, Elton, Youlgreave, Castleton, Hathersage.
Bed & Breakfast — Matlock Bath, Bonsall, Winster, Elton, Youlgeave, Monyash, Ashford in the Water, Great Longstone, Stoney Middleton, Eyam, Great Hucklow, Castleton, Bradwell.
Inns — numerous on the route and of particular mining note are the Pig of Lead at Bonsall and the Miners Standard at Winster.

BONSALL CROSS & THE KING'S HEAD INN

ODIN MINE CRUSHING CIRCLE, NR CASTLETON

THE ROACHES

BEESTON TOR, MANIFOLD VALLEY

PEAK DISTRICT HIGH LEVEL ROUTE — 90 MILES

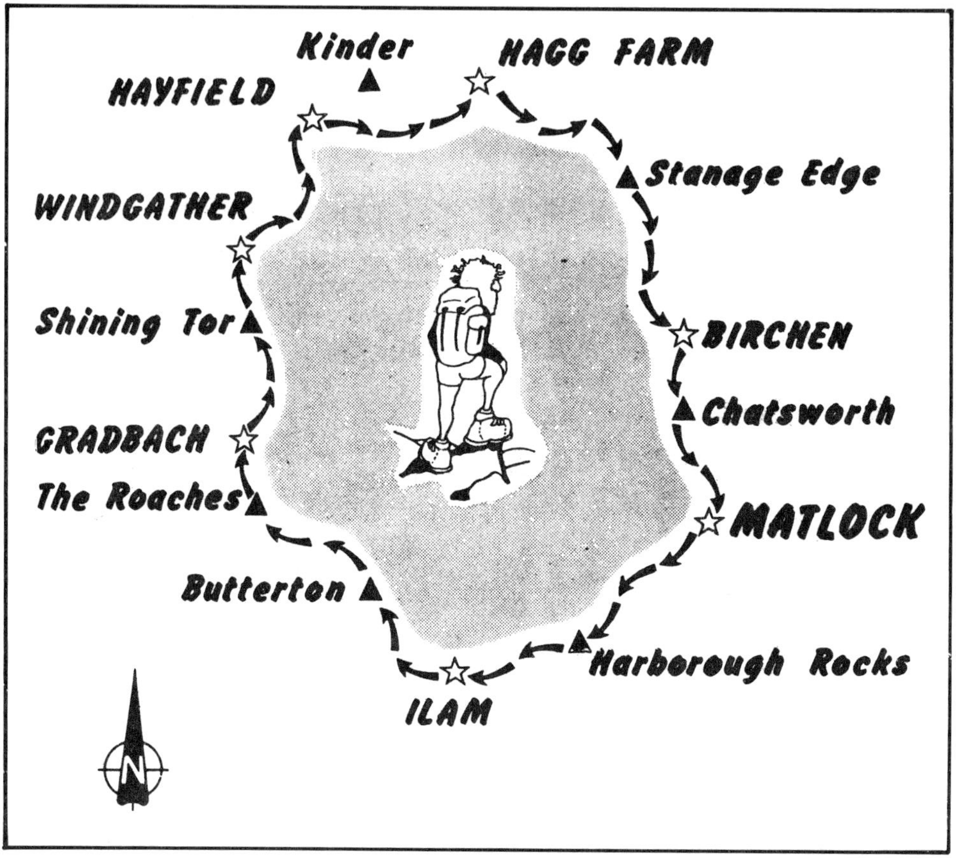

THREE SHIRES HEAD

PEAK DISTRICT : HIGH LEVEL ROUTE
90 Miles - Circular

Encircling the Peak District from Matlock.

Devised, created and inaugurated by John Merrill in September 1983.

Because of the geological make-up of the Peak District, we have a limestone inner and a gritstone rim. Using the rim as a base I worked out a route which kept to as much high ground as possible, away from villages and the normal long distance routes. Although I am biased, the walk is a superb one with magnificent views all the time. It is a hard walk and on my final inauguration I took four days, but it can be comfortably walked in six days. There are numerous campsites, hostels, accomodation, and some twenty inns along the way!

The route keeps to the highest and most rugged parts as it weaves its way from Matlock across the limestone plateau to Dove Dale. Here it heads north to the Roaches and Shining Tor. The northern end traverses Chinley Churn before crossing the southern edge of Kinder to Ladybower Reservoir. The eastern side follows the whole of the gritstone edge system from Stanage to Beeley before descending to the river Derwent and the final four miles back to Matlock.

ROUTE OUTLINE
Matlock - Bonsall - Harborough Rocks - Brassington - Tissington - Thorpe - Dove Dale - Ilam - Calton - Grindon - Butterton - Mermaid Inn - Upper Hulme - The Roaches - Gradbach - Three Shires Head - Cat & Fiddle Inn - Shining Tor - Cats Tor - Windgather - Taxal - Whaley Bridge - Buxworth - Chinley Churn - Hayfield - Edale Cross - Grindsbrook - Crookstone Knoll - Hagg Farm - Crook Hill - Ladybower Reservoir - Stanage Edge - Millstone Edge - Longshaw - Froggatt Edge - Curbar Edge - Baslow Edge - Birchens Edge - Chatsworth Edge - Hunting Tower - Swiss Lake - Beeley Hilltop - Fallange - Northwood - River Derwent - Oaker - Matlock.

MAPS
O.S. 1:25,000 Outdoor Leisure Map - The White Peak
O.S. 1.25,000 Outdoor Leisure Map - The Dark Peak
O.S. 1:50,000 Sheet No. 110 - Sheffield & Huddersfield.

GUIDEBOOK —
Peak District: High Level Route John N. Merrill JNM Publications 1987

BADGE AND COMPLETION CERTIFICATE —
A four colour embroidered badge on a black cloth together with a signed certificate is available from JNM Publications.

ACCOMODATION - on or close to the route -
Bed and Breakfast - Matlock, Brassington, Thorpe, Butterson, Upper Hulme, Gradbach, Kettleshulme, Hayfield, Edale, Hathersage, Baslow, Beeley.
Youth Hostels - Matlock, Ilam, Gradbach, Edale, Hagg Farm, Hathersage.
Camping sites - Thorpe, Ilam, Bradbach, Hayfield, Hagg Farm, Hathersage, Birchens Edge, Darley Bridge.

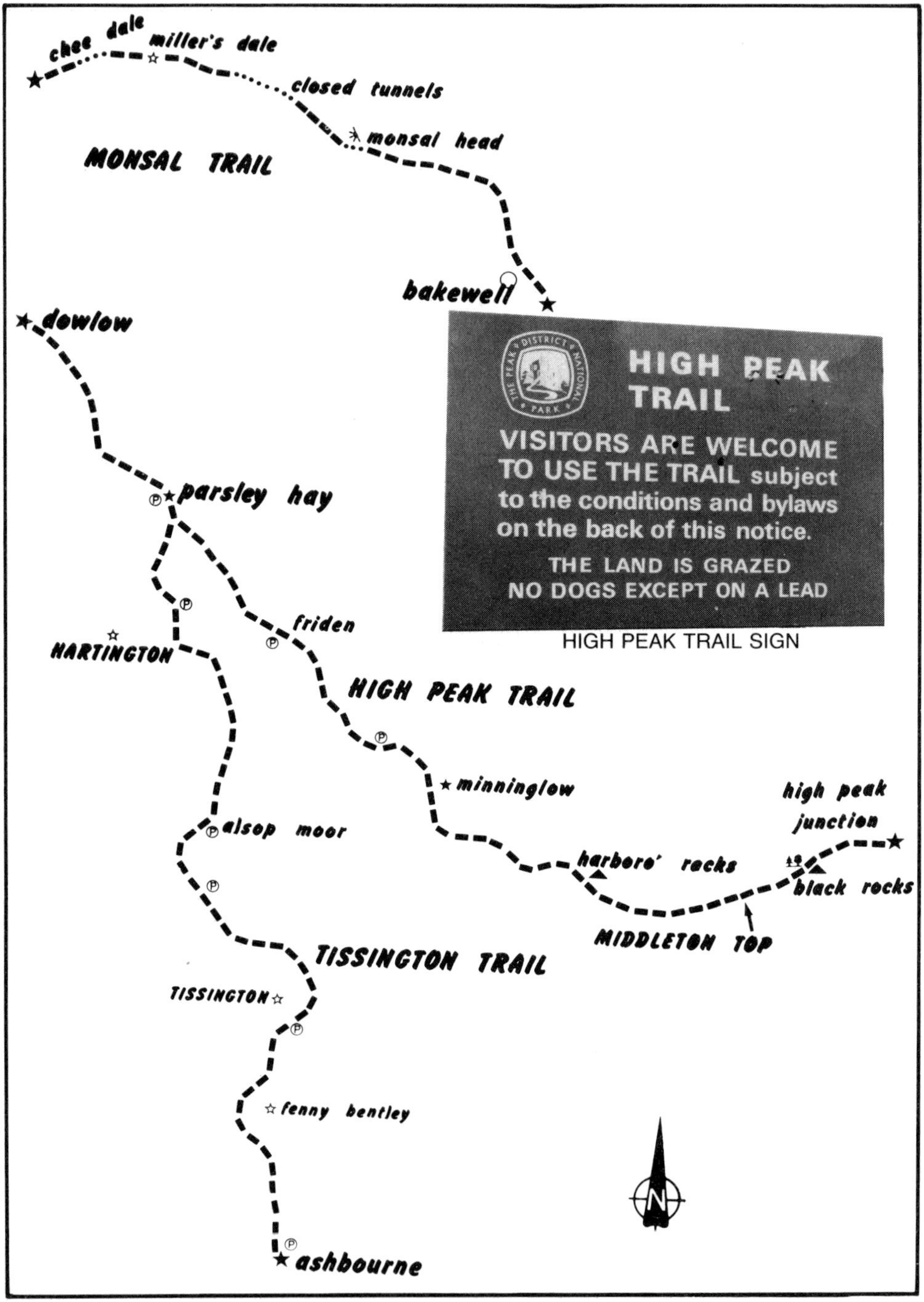

HIGH PEAK TRAIL SIGN

DERBYSHIRE TRAILS

The 1970's have seen a major development of reclaiming disused railway lines and converting them to bridleways. While they are naturally level walking, they do open a new area of walking in the Peak District. Car parks have been created at the old railway stations, cycle hire schemes and bus services have been introduced for the summer months.

They provide the motorist and short distance walker with a new series of walks, but they also give the serious walker several new middle distance walks.

The Trails are through tunnels, along embankments, over bridges and through cuttings, and have been created by the Peak Park Planning Board.

1. TISSINGTON TRAIL - 13 miles - Ashbourne to Parsley Hay.
   Opened in 1971-2.
2. HIGH PEAK TRAIL - 17½ miles - High Peak Junction to Dowlow, near Buxton.
   Opened in 1972.
3. MONSAL TRAIL - 8 miles - Coombs Road Viaduct to Blackwell Mill Cottages.
   Opened in 1981.
   Three major tunnels are closed, and link paths join the Trail together.

MAPS
1:25,000 O.S. Outdoor Leisure Map - The White Peak.
1:50,000 O.S. Sheet No. 119 - Buxton, Matlock and Dovedale.

GUIDEBOOK
Derbyshire Trails by John N. Merrill. Dalesman 1980.

ACCOMMODATION
Camp Sites - Monyash, Ashbourne and Alstonfield.
Youth Hostels - Matlock Bath, Elton, Buxton, Hartington, Bakewell and Ravenstor.
Bed and Breakfast - Cromford, Matlock Bath, Monyash, Hartington, Ashbourne and Monsal Head.

HIGH PEAK TRAIL

THE SETT VALLEY TRAIL — 3 MILES

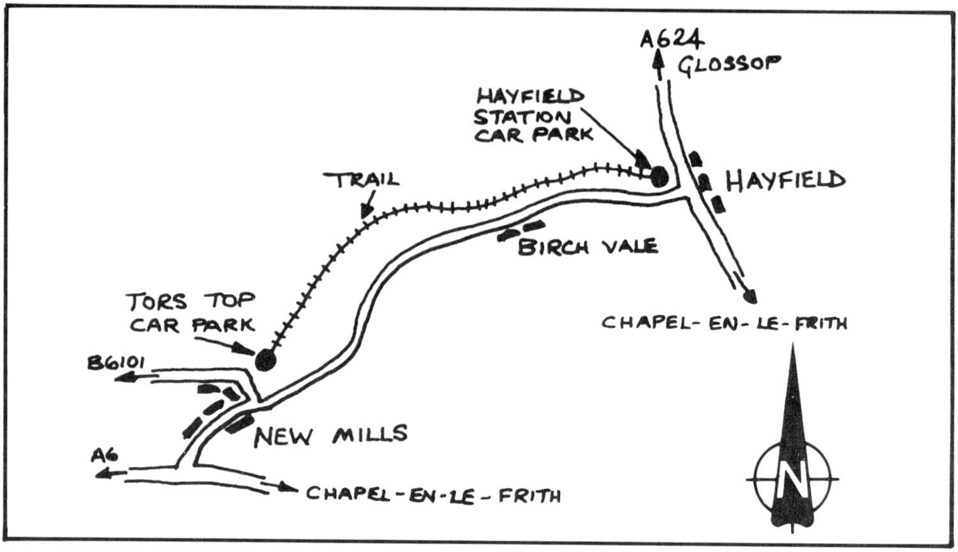

From New Mills to Hayfield.

The Trail is along an old railway line that was built in the 1860's at a cost of £27,040. Although made for two tracks, only one was laid. On March 1st 1868, the first passenger service began, and on January 3rd 1970, the branch line was closed. ive years later the Derbyshire County Council began converting the old line into a pedestrian way with car parks at either end. In 1976 it was opened to the public. A walk along the trail links two very interesting towns together, rich in industrial archaeology, whilst above towers the mass of Kinder and its bleak moorlands.

MAPS —

O.S. 1;50,000 Sheet No 110 — Sheffield and Huddersfield
O.S. 1:25,000 Outdoor Leisure map — The Dark Peak

WINNATS PASS

EIGHT OTHER WALKS

1. **THREE TUNNEL WALK** - Over the tops of Cowburn, Woodhead and Diggle tunnels. From Chapel en le Frith to Diggle; about 35 miles.
Originator - Neil Ross. Date unknown.

MAP
1:50,000 O.S. Sheet No. 110 - Sheffield and Huddersfield.
1:25,000 O.S. Outdoor Leisure Map - The Dark Peak.

2. **HORSESHOE OF THE PEAK** - 63 miles - Inaugurated by R. E. Lambe and John Sumner - 29th/30th August, 1952. Time: 37 hrs. 10 mins. (28 hours of actual walking).
The route keeps to the gritstone country, completing a horseshoe around the Peak District limestone country.

ROUTE OUTLINE
Hen Cloud - Combs Moss - Colbourne - Edale Cross - Kinder Downfall - Doctor's Gate - Wain Stones - Grinah Stones - Featherbed Moss - Abbey Brook - Stanage Edge - Burbage - Longshaw - Froggatt Edge - Birchen's Edge - Chatsworth Park - Beeley Moor - Matlock Railway Station.

MAPS
1.50,000 O.S. Sheet Nos. 119 - Buxton, Matlock and Dovedale.
110 - Sheffield and Huddersfield.
1:25,000 O.S. Outdoor Leisure Map - The Dark Peak.

3. **THREE RIVERS WALK** - 53 miles - Originated by R. E. Lambe in 1956.

ROUTE OUTLINE
Rushton Spencer - River Dane - River Manifold - River Dove - Axe Edge.
The route follows the entire length of each river.

On the original 'solo' walk, R. E. Lambe planned to include the River Wye - adding another 25 miles - by continuing from Axe Edge to Buxton and down the Wye to Rowsley. He sprained his ankle, and experienced appalling weather on the walk, so he stopped at Axe Edge. The walk can be further extended to include a fifth river - the Derwent - to Bleaklow.

MAPS
1:50,000 O.S. Sheet Nos. 118 - The Potteries.
119 - Buxton, Matlock and Dovedale.
1:25,000 O.S. Outdoor Leisure Map - The White Peak.

4. **COLNE ROWSLEY** - 73 miles. Inaugurated by Fred Heardman, Harold Gerrard and John Burton in March 1926 in 27½ hours.

ROUTE OUTLINE
Colne - Hebden Bridge - Marsden - Isle of Skye Inn - Black Hill - Dunford Bridge - Cutgate - Abbey Brook - Ladybower - Stanage Edge - Longshaw - Froggatt Edge - Chatsworth - Rowsley.
Has now been extended to Matlock, making it 75 miles long and completed in under 24 hours. First Winter crossing in December 1952.

Colne - Rowsley—continued

MAPS
1:25,000 O.S. Outdoor Leisure Map - The Dark Peak.
1:50,000 O.S. Sheet Nos. 103 - Blackburn and Burnley.
109 - Manchester.
110 - Sheffield and Huddersfield.
119 - Buxton, Matlock and Dovedale.

5. **COLNE - BUXTON** - 51 miles. Inaugurated by Dawson, Frank and Harry Summersgill. The route from Colne takes in Hebden Bridge, Blackstone Edge, Marsden and the Three Inns Walk.

In 1918 Eustace Thomas and Norman Begg did the walk in 17 hours 57 minutes. In 1919 Harry Phillips extended the walk to Ashbourne.

MAPS
1:25,000 O.S. Outdoor Leisure Map - The Dark Peak.
1:50,000 O.S. Sheet Nos. 103 - Blackburn and Burnley.
109 - Manchester.
110 - Sheffield and Huddersfield.
119 - Buxton, Matlock and Dovedale.

6. **TWO INNS WALK** - 120 miles. Links the two highest Inns in England together - Tan Hill in Yorkshire (1,732 ft.) and Cat & Fiddle near Buxton (1,690 ft.) completed 5th/7th June 1952 as a non-stop walk. V.J. Desmond took 54 hrs. 10 mins. His companions, Williamson and Courtenay, arrived 1½ hours later.

This high level route includes - Great Shunner Fell, Buckden Pike, Great Whernside, Todmorden, Marsden, Black Hill, Bleaklow, Kinder, Edale, Castle Naze and Long Hill.

MAPS
1:50,000 O.S. Sheet Nos. 98 - Wensleydale and Wharfedale.
103 - Blackburn and Burnley.
109 - Manchester.
110 - Buxton, Matlock and Dovedale.

7. **THE DUFFIELD SKYLINE** - 10 miles - Devised by Lionel Bailey.
A short circular walk in south Derbyshire taking high ground and crossing the Derwent and Ecclesbourne valleys.
Basic Route - Duffield - Little Eaton - Milford - Hazlewood - Ecclesbourne River - Duffield.

MAP
1:50,000 O.S. Sheet No. 119 - Buxton, Matlock and Dovedale.
Details and guide sheet from: Lionel W. Bailey, 69 Park Road, Duffield, Derby, DE6 4GR.

8. **BULLOCK SMITHY HIKE** - 56 miles - Held annually in September is this organised tough 24 hr. challenge walk in the northern Peak District. The walk involves more than 7,000 feet of ascent. In 1983 248 people started but 80 retired en route. The winners were Les Stephenson and David Cunningham in a new record time of 8 hrs. 38 mins. The first lady - Pauline Calder - took 13 hrs. 40 mins.

Details from: Fielding Lord, 89 Bramhill Moor Lane, Hazel Grove, Stockport, Cheshire.

FROGGATT PINNACLE AND EDGE

QUIET WOMAN INN, EARL STERNDALE

A CESTRIAN LINK WALK - 120 Miles

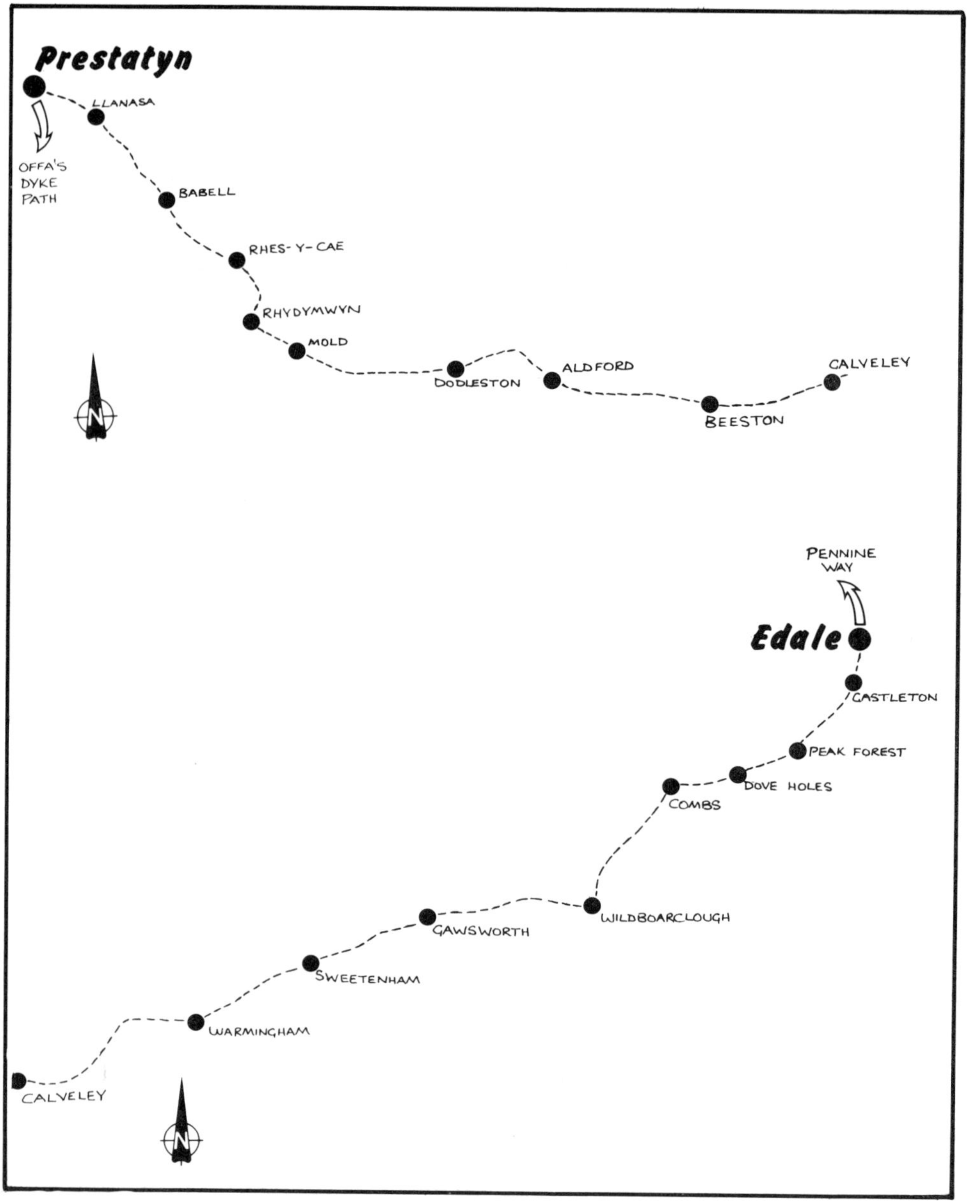

A CESTRIAN LINK WALK - 120 Miles

Devised by John N. Davenport.

A route linking the northern end of Offa's Dyke Path to the southern end of the Pennine Way.

The route makes an excellent link to Offa's Dyke and the Pennine Way and can be walked in its own right through delightful and unspoilt countryside. On both my 2,000 mile walk linking the ten National Parks and footpaths together and my 1,600 mile Land's End - John o' Groats walk. I too walked from Offa's Dyke to the Pennine Way and the basic line follows similar ground. The principal section is across Cheshire; hence the walks name; and walking in Cheshire is very understimated. Whilst it may not have rugged mountains the countryside is attractive and full of history. Amongst the highlights is Beeston Castle which gives extensive views over the Cheshire Plain.

BASIC ROUTE
Prestatyn - Llansa - Trelogan - Babell - Lixwm - Rhosemor - Rhydymwyn - Mold - Leeswood - Dodleston - Eccleston - Aldford - Tattenhall - Beeston - Bunbury - Calveley - Church Minshull - Warmingham - Swettenham - Marton - Gawsworth - Wildboarclough - Combs - Dove Holes - Peak Forest - Castleton - Edale.

MAPS
1:50,000 O.S. Sheet Nos. 116 - Denbigh and Colwyn Bay.
117 - Chester.
118 - The Potteries.
119 - Buxton, Matlock and Dove Dale.
110 - Sheffield and Huddersfield.

GUIDEBOOK
A Cestrian Link Walk by John N. Davenport. Westmorland Gazette 1983.

ACCOMODATION
Youth Hostels - Maeshafn, Chester, Gradbach, Buxton, Castleton and Edale.
Bed and Breakfast - Prestatyn, Whitford, Babell, Lixwm, Rhes-y-Cae, Rhosemor, Rhydymwyn, Mold, Pontblyddyn, Rossett, Pulford, Eccleston, Chester, Tarporley, Middlewich, Elworth, Sandbach, Cleulow Cross, Macclesfield Forest, Combs, Chapel-en-le-Frith, Dove Holes, Peak Forest, Castleton, Edale.

NAGS HEAD INN, EDALE

SANDSTONE TRAIL — 32 MILES

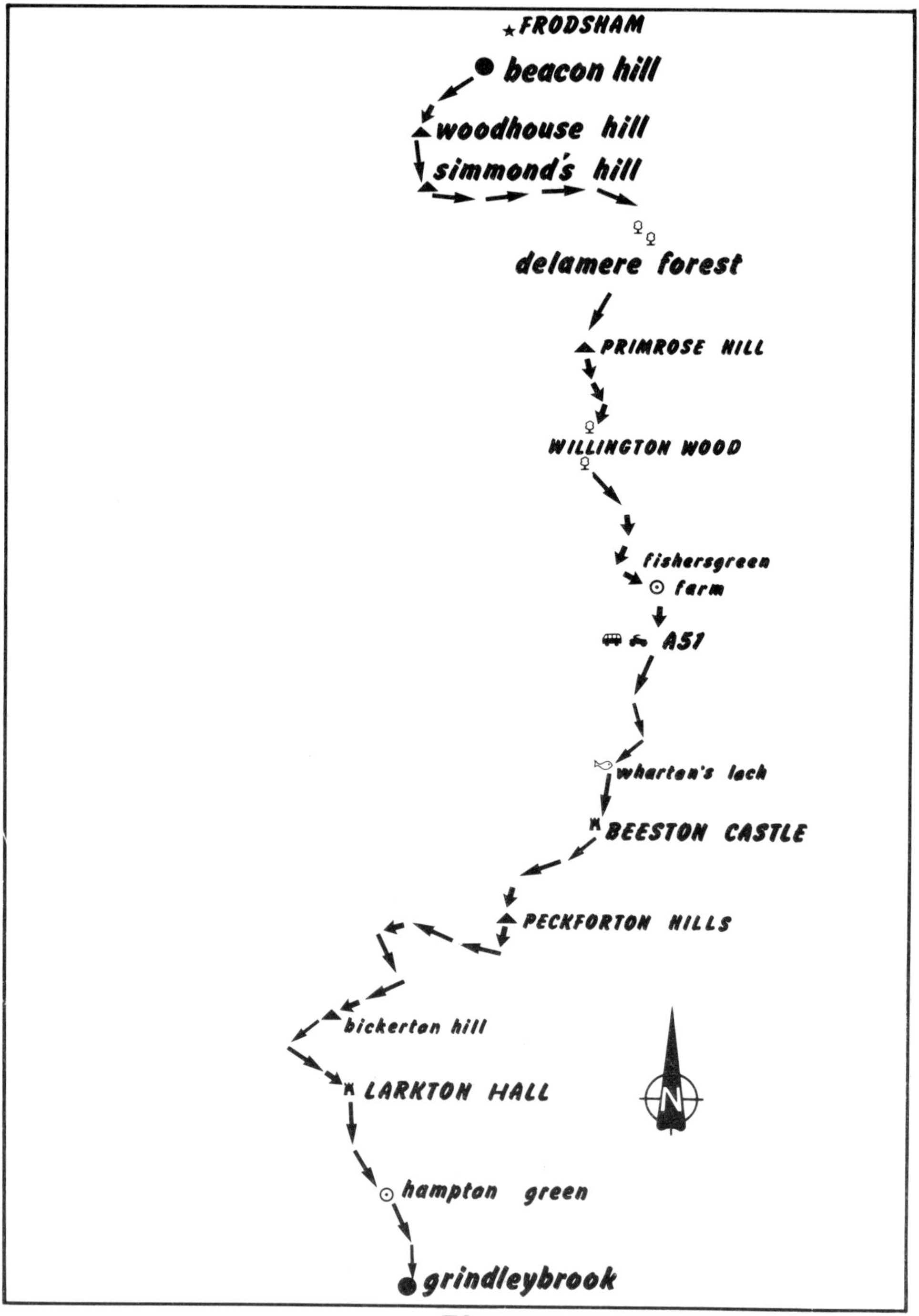

SANDSTONE TRAIL — 32 Miles

Beacon Hill to Grindley Brook

Developed by the Countryside and Recreation Division of the Cheshire County Council. Although far from the Peak District border, it is a companion walk to the Gritstone Trail, and being on its own it deserves including in this book's survey. I first came across this route on a 2,000 mile walk of England and Wales in 1976. At Beeston Castle I kept seeing yellow waymarks with the letter 'S' on a boot imprint, and wondered what it was.

Situated in Cheshire, the route loosely follows the sandstone ridge and very rarely attains more than 700 feet above sea level. The Trail passes through attractive scenery, full of history, from the Cheshire Plains to rocky outcrops and wooded hills. Again the walk can be done as a challenge in a day or over two days. The route is usually walked north to south.

ROUTE OUTLINE
Beacon Hill (Frodsham) - Woodhouse Hill - Simmonds Hill - Manley Common - Delamere Forest - Primrose Hill - Willington Wood - Fishers Green - Ferney Lees - Shropshire Union Canal - Beeston Castle - Peckforton Wood - Bulkeley Hill - Bickerton Hill - Maiden Castle - Larkton Hall - Broomy Bank - Bickley Hall - Pearl Farm - Willeymoor Lock, Shropshire Union Canal - Grindley Brook.

MAP
1:50,000 O.S. Sheet No. 117 - Chester.

GUIDEBOOK
Sandstone Trail - Walker's Guide - Cheshire County Council. (includes O.S. strip maps).

BEESTON CASTLE

GRITSTONE TRAIL — 18 1/2 MILES

WHITE NANCY

GRITSTONE TRAIL — 18½ Miles

Lyme Park to Rushton

Developed by the Countryside and Recreation Division of the Cheshire County Council.

Located along the western edge of the Peak District, the Trail traverses the "hilly" country of Cheshire. The whole trail is well signed with an arrowed footprint with the letter 'G'. The walk can be completed in its entirety, starting from either end, in a day or in sections using Tegg's Nose Country Park as a base. The route provides distant views, is rich in history, and passes through very attractive scenery. The southern terminus - Rushton - is on the Cheshire/Staffordshire border, the start of the Staffordshire Way and the Mow Cop Trail.

ROUTE OUTLINE
Lyme Park - Sponds Hill - Cheshire Hunt Inn - White Nancy - Cow Lane Mill - Gorsey Brow - Teggs Nose Country Park - Bottoms Reservoir - Bollin Head Farm - Lowerhouse - Croker Hills - A54 - Wincle Minn - Hawkslee Farm - Barleyford - A523.

MAPS
1:50,000 O.S. Sheet Nos. 109 - Manchester.
118 - The Potteries.
1:25,000 O.S. Outdoor Leisure Map - The White Peak. Shows part of route clearly marked.

GUIDEBOOK
Gritstone Trail - Walker's Guide - Cheshire Country Council. (Has O.S. strip maps).

GRITSTONE TRAIL SIGN

THE MIDDLEWOOD WAY — 11 MILES

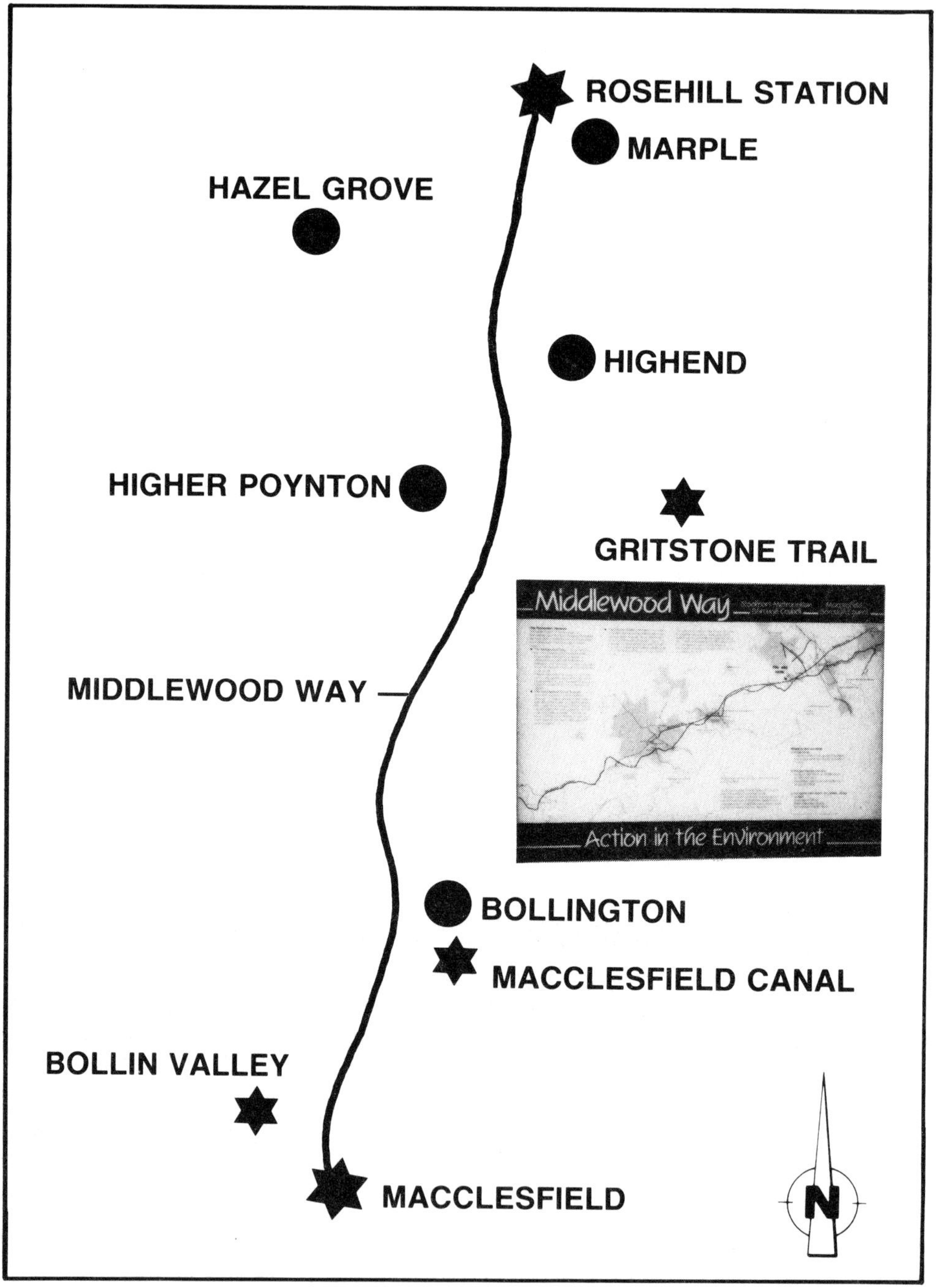

THE MIDDLEWOOD WAY — 11 MILES

— From Hurdsfield, Macclesfield in the south to Rose Hill, Marple in the north.

The M,B and M railway — Macclesfield, Bollington and Marple — was built in the 1860's and a hundred years later in 1970 it closed to passenger and goods trains. A few years later the Macclesfield Borough and Stockport Metropolitan Borough Councils began converting the line into an ammenity. In 1985 it was opened to walkers, cyclists and riders, with separate paths for each and car parks at various places along its route. The way is through a particularly attractive area and can be linked to several other routes in the area of Cheshire, notably the Bollin Valley, Ladybrook Valley, the Gritsone Trail and the Macclesfield Canal. The permutations are numerous!

MAPS —

O.S. 1:50,000 — Sheet No 109 — Manchester
O.S. 1:50,000 — Sheet No 118 — The Potteries
O.S. 1:25,000 — Sheet SJ87/97 — Macclesfield & Alderley Edge
O.S. 1:25,000 — Sheet SJ88/98

LEAFLET —

Middlewood Way published jointly by the Macclesfield Borough Council, Stockport Metropolitan Borough Council, and Cheshire County Council.

MIDDLEWOOD WAY

THE STAFFORDSHIRE WAY — 92 MILES

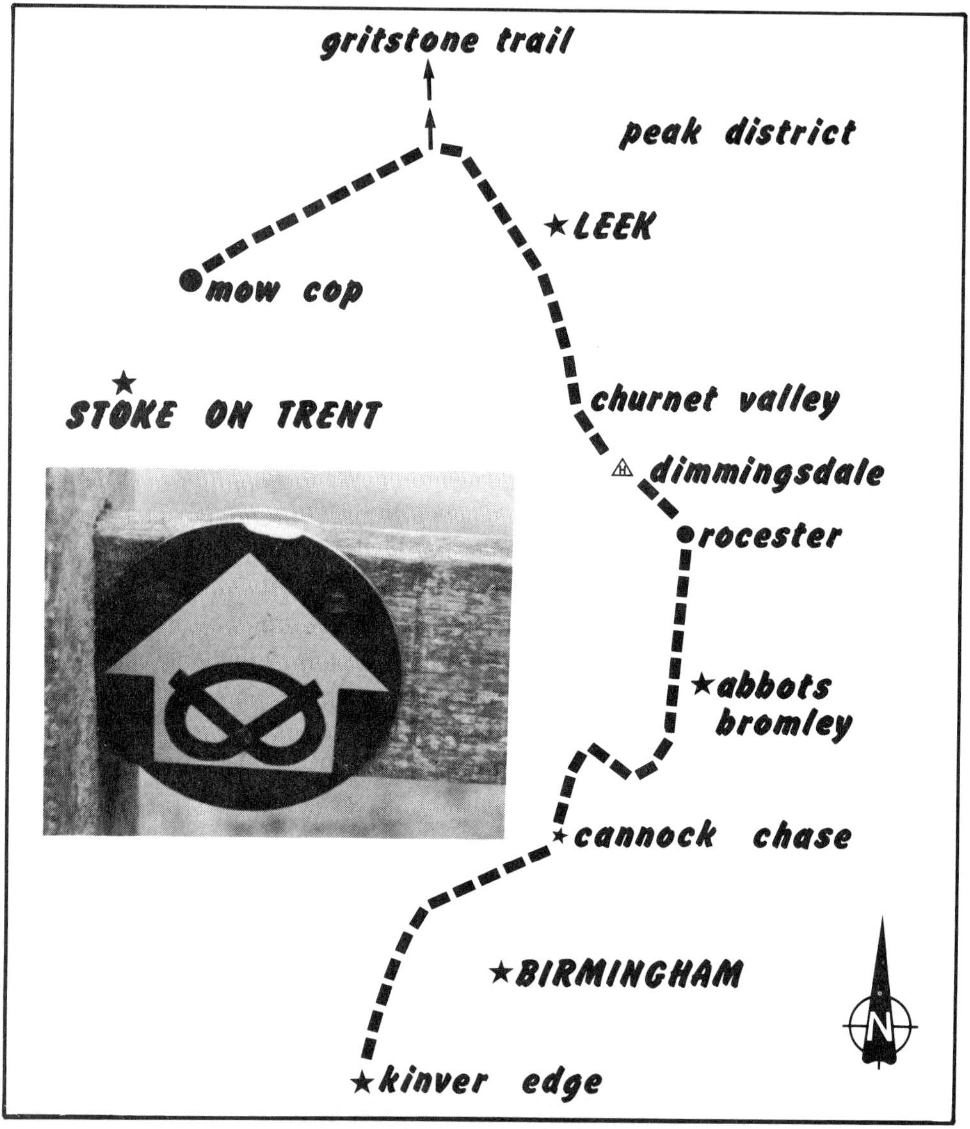

STAFFORDSHIRE WAY SIGN

THE STAFFORDSHIRE WAY — 92 MILES

Mow Cop to Kinver Edge

Created by the Staffordshire County Council. Completed in 1982.

The route weaves its way round the southern end of the Peak District and beautiful Churnet Valley before heading southwards to Rocester and the River Dore. Leaving the hilly country behind, the Way passes close to Uttoxeter and Abbots Bromley to Cannock Chase. The final thirty miles are to Kinver Edge. It is possible to extend the walk by using the Gritstone Trail and the West Midland Way - making it possible to walk from the Southern side of Manchester to Birmingham (Kinver Edge). From here it is possible to follow the North Worcestershire Path — 26 miles — to Forhill. The Worcester County Council have proposed a Worcestershire Way from Kinver Edge to the Malvern Hills. On the way this could link in with the Cotswold Way. At Cannock Chase it is possible to link in with the Heart Of England Way — 80 miles through Warwickshire. The permutations are countless!

The whole route is well signposted, with a yellow or blue arrow incorporating a Staffordshire knot symbol. The Staffordshire County Council have recently produced a leaflet about the way complete with detailed accomodation list, enabling you to either bed and breadfast or backpack the route. The only Youth Hostel is at Dimmingsdale in the Churnet Valley.

MAPS
1:50,000 O.S. Sheet Nos. 118 - The Potteries.
128 - Derby and Burton-upon-Trent.
127 - Stafford and Telford.

GUIDEBOOKS

1. Mow Cop to Rocester — 32 miles
2. Rochester to Cannock Chase — 25 miles
3. Cannock Chase to Kinver Edge — 35 miles

All guides include detailed strip maps based on the Ordnance Survey maps. The guides are published by the Staffordshire County Council's, County Planning and Development Dept in Stafford.

ALTON AND THE CHURNET VALLEY

THE MOW COP TRAIL — 9 MILES

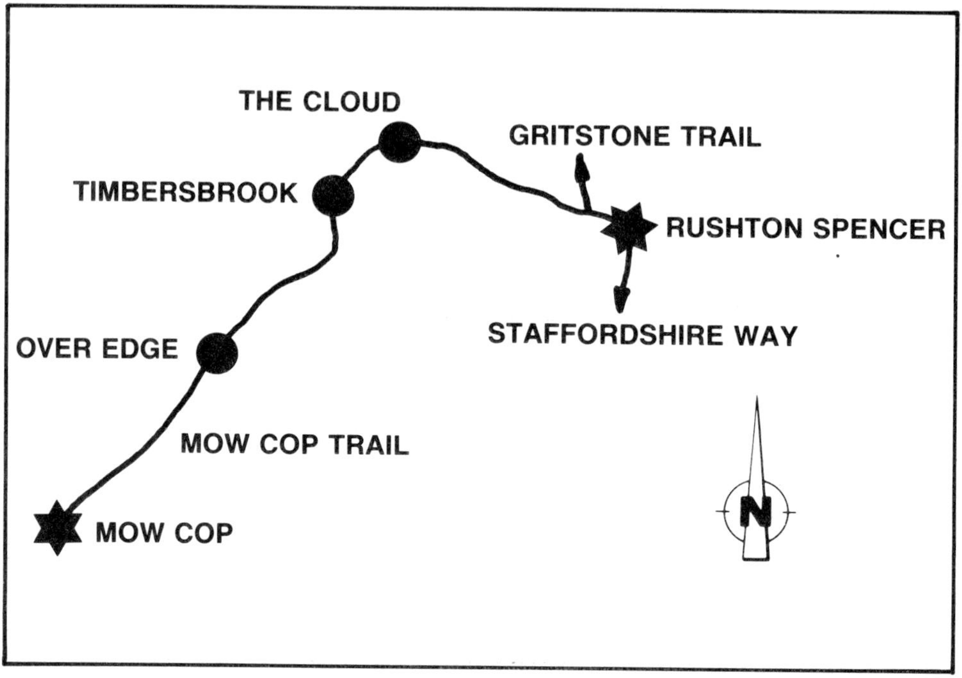

THE CLOUD & MACCLESFIELD CANAL

THE MOW COP TRAIL — 9 Miles

Starting at the folly at 1,100 feet, with a sensational view over the Cheshire plain the trail heads north easterly to Rushton Spencer. Here you can continue along the Staffordshire Way or head northwards along the Gritstone Trail. Although a short trail the walk passes through very pleasant scenery and is a very enjoyable walk in its own right. Much of the time you have views over the plain and the summit of The Cloud is exceptional with the Macclesfield Canal below. Like the other Cheshire trails it is well waymarked and in this instance with a yellow arrow with a black M.

ROUTE —

Mow Cop — Whitemoor Farm — Overedge — Timbersbrook — The Cloud — Raven's Clough — Rushton Spencer.

MAPS —

O.S. 1:50,000 Sheet No 118 — The Potteries
O.S. 1:25,000 Sheet No SJ 86/96 — Congleton
O.S. 1:25,000 Sheet No SJ 85/95 — Kidsgrove and Leek.

GUIDEBOOK —

Mow Cop Trail — Walker's Guide Cheshire County Council

MOW COP FOLLY

CANALS

For a long while I felt that the canal system in the area had been overlooked by the walking public and in 1986 began ammeding the situation by writing my first Canal Walk book — Vol One — Derbyshire and Nottinghamshire. The walking in the main is flat, largely through unspolit and attractive scenery rich in history. Following the canals you can see for yourself the "motorway system of the 18th century". You walk along the towpaths past locks, cuttings, over aqueducts, through tunnels, and past numerous inns! I have just recently completed Vol Two, covering canals in Cheshire and Staffordshire, which required more than 500 miles of walking to do justice to te potential that exists. Whilst both books describe circular walks of varying lengths I have also mentioned that each canal can be walked end to end as a 'challenge' walk or as a weekend walk. I offer them as an extension to the long walks already described in this book and I hope that you walk along the towpaths and see for yourself their attractive qualities.

Chesterfield Canal — Worksop to West Stockwith — 26 miles
Erewash Canal — Langley Mill to River Trent — 11½ miles
Peak Forest Canal — Whaley Bridge to Ashton Canal — 14¾ miles
Macclesfield Canal — Marple to Bull Bridge — 27¾ miles
Caldon Canal — Froghall to Etruria — 17 miles

The complete 97 miles of the Cheshire Ring makes a really fascinating walk and I am currently working on a guidebook to it.

GUIDEBOOKS

Canal Walks Vol One — Derbyshire and Nottinghamshire John N. Merrill JNM Publications 1986
Canal Walks Vol Two — Cheshire and Staffordshire John N. Merrill JNM Publications 1987

JOHN MERRILL'S CANAL WALK BADGE

— a four colour embroidered badge of a lock gate on a blue cloth. From JNM Publications, and only available to walkers who have completed at least six of his canal walks from his Canal Walk Guide series.

PEAK FOREST CANAL

MACCLESFIELD CANAL

PUBLICITY WORKS & MACCLESFIELD CANAL

OTHER JOHN MERRILL CHALLENGE WALKS

JOHN MERRILL'S YORKSHIRE DALES CHALLENGE WALK — 23 miles

Circular walk starting from Kettlewell, in the heart of the Dales. The walk is a challenge to complete within twelve hours and invlives 3,600 feet of ascent while encompassing the scenic variety to be found in the National Park — mountains, moorlands, limestone country and dale walking.

ROUTE —

Kettlewell — Buckden Pike — Cray — Deepdale — Beckermonds — Halton Gill — Litton — Arncliffe — Kettlewell.

MAPS —

O.S. 1:25,000 Outdoor Leisure Map — Malham and Upper Wharfedale
O.S. 1:25,000 Outdoor Leisure Map — Yorkshire Dales

GUIDEBOOK —

John Merrill's Yorkshire Dales Challenge Walk John N. Merrill JNM Publications 1986

BADGES AND CERTIFICATES —

A four colour embroidered badge on a red cloth is available with certificate from JNM Publications.

JOHN MERRILL'S NORTH YORKSHIRE MOORS CHALLENGE WALK — 24 MILES

A seaside bash! Circular walk from Goathland in the heart of the moors. The route combines moorland, river valley and coastal walking, using Robin Hood's Bay as the half — way point, and involves 2,000 feet of ascent.

ROUTE —

Goathland — Sleights Moor — Little Beck — Raw — Robin Hood's Bay — Fyingdales Moor — Falling Foss — Goathland.

MAP —

O.S. Outdoor Leisure Map — North Yorkshire Moors — Eastern area

GUIDEBOOK —

John Merrill's North Yorkshire Moors Challenge Walk John N. Merrill JNM Publications 1986

BADGE AND COMPLETION CERTIFICATE —

A four colour embroidered badge on a green cloth is available with certificate from JNM Publications.

FORTHCOMING TITLES —

John Merrill's Lakeland Challenge Walk
John Merrill's Dark Peak Challenge Walk

THE JOHN MERRILL WALK BADGE —

As many people have now walked more than two of his walks or done one of them at least twice a special four colour embroidered circular badge on a black cloth is available from JNM Publications.

JOHN MERRILL CHALLENGE WALK BADGES & CERTIFICATES

ORGANISATIONS CONCERNED WITH LONG DISTANCE WALKING.

THE INTERNATIONAL VOLKSSPORT VERBAND — G.B. FEDERATION.

The organisation was founded in 1968 by walking clubs in Germany, Austria, Switzerland and Leichtenstein. They felt there was a need for walking events whereby the entrants could walk at their own pace — "the sole aim to enjoy themselves." The headquarters are in Munich and there are now organisations in many countries throughout Europe and the world. In 1983 there were 4,500 individual clubs, with 5,300 events and more than 14,500,000 people taking part. The events are held with basic aims of furthering international friendship through healthy exercise that the whole family can participate in.

The British organisation now has more than 40 clubs and a full calendar of walks throughout the year — the Bolsover District Walk is one. The more serious walker can participate in many of the events and record his walks in Record Books. Many get their books stamped earning themselves awards for the number of events particiapted in and number of kilometers walked. For fuller details of the IVV and the walks contact-
G. Walker,
Publicity Officer — North,
14, Strathmore Drive,
Baildon,
Bradford.
West Yorkshire
BD17 5LP

THE LONG DISTANCE WALKERS ASSOCIATION

Founded in 1972 to satisfy the growing interest in long distance walking in Britain on official and unofficial long distance routes, and challenge walks. The membership is now over 4,000 with numerous local groups throughout the country. Members recieve the association's journal, "Strider", published several times during the year, detailing the dates of challenge walks, local group activities, and news of new routes. Details from the Membership Secretary –
4 Mayfield Road,
Tunbridge Wells,
Kent,
TN4 8ES

SUGGESTED FURTHER READING

HIGH PEAK
by Eric Byne and Geoffrey Sutton. Secker & Warburg. 1966.

DARK PEAK WRECKS
by Ron Collier and Ron Wilkinson Barnsley Chronicle. 1979.

PORTRAIT OF THE PENNINES
by Roger Redfern. Robert Hale.

FREEDOM TO ROAM.
by Howard Hill. Moorland Publishing. 1980.

THE 1932 KINDER TRESPASS
by Benny Rothman Willow Publishing. 1982.

GUIDEBOOK PUBLISHERS ADDRESSES

Thornhill Press,
24 Moorend Road,
Cheltenham,
Gloucestershire.

Cheshire County Council,
Countryside and Recreation Dept.,
County Hall,
Chester.

J. N. M. Publications,
Winster,
Matlock,
Derbyshire.
DE4 2DQ.

Dalesman Publishing Co. Ltd.
Clapham,
Via Lancaster,
North Yorkshire.

Staffordshire County Council,
Planning Dept.,
Martin Street,
Stafford.

Westmorland Gazette,
22 Stricklandgate,
Kendal,
Cumbria.

OTHER BOOKS BY JOHN N. MERRILL PUBLISHED BY JNM PUBLICATIONS

DAY WALK GUIDES —

SHORT CIRCULAR WALKS IN THE PEAK DISTRICT
LONG CIRCULAR WALKS IN THE PEAK DISTRICT
CIRCULAR WALKS IN WESTERN PEAKLAND
SHORT CIRCULAR WALKS IN THE STAFFORDSHIRE MOORLANDS
PEAK DISTRICT TOWN WALKS
SHORT CIRCULAR WALKS AROUND MATLOCK
SHORT CIRCULAR WALKS IN THE DUKERIES
SHORT CIRCULAR WALKS IN SOUTH YORKSHIRE
CIRCULAR WALKS AROUND DERBY
HIKE TO BE FIT....STROLLING WITH JOHN
THE JOHN MERRILL WALK RECORD BOOK

CANAL WALK GUIDES —

VOL ONE — DERBYSHIRE AND NOTTINGHAMSHIRE
VOL TWO — CHESHIRE AND STAFFORDSHIRE

DAY CHALLENGE WALKS —

JOHN MERRILL'S PEAK DISTRICT CHALLENGE WALK
JOHN MERRILL'S YORKSHIRE DALES CHALLENGE WALK
JOHN MERRILL'S NORTH YORKSHIRE MOORS CHALLENGE WALK
PEAK DISTRICT END TO END WALKS
THE LITTLE JOHN CHALLENGE WALK
JOHN MERRILL'S LAKELAND CHALLENGE WALK

MULTIPLE DAY WALKS —

THE RIVERS' WAY
PEAK DISTRICT HIGH LEVEL ROUTE
PEAK DISTRICT MARATHONS
THE LIMEY WAY
THE PEAKLAND WAY

HISTORICAL GUIDES —

DERBYSHIRE INNS
100 HALLS AND CASTLES OF THE PEAK DISTRICT & DERBYSHIRE
TOURING THE PEAK DISTRICT AND DERBYSHIRE BY CAR
DERBYSHIRE FOLKLORE
LOST INDUSTRIES OF DERBYSHIRE
PUNISHMENT IN DERBYSHIRE
CUSTOMS OF THE PEAK DISTRICT AND DERBYSHIRE
WINSTER — A VISITOR'S GUIDE
ARKWRIGHT OF CROMFORD
TALES FROM THE MINES by GEOFFREY CARR

JOHN'S MARATHON WALKS —

TURN RIGHT AT LAND'S END
WITH MUSTARD ON MY BACK
TURN RIGHT AT DEATH VALLEY
EMERALD COAST WALK

JOHN N. MERILL ON DERBYSHIRE BOUNDARY WALK

WALK RECORD CHART

Date walked

SOUTH YORKSHIRE —

ROTHERHAM ROUND WALK — 25 MILES ....

SHEFFIELD ROUND WALK — 10 MILES...

THE SHEFFIELD WAY — 45 MILES..

CAL-DER-WENT WALK — 30 MILES..

NOTTINGHAMSHIRE —

THE LITTLE JOHN CHALLENGE WALK — 28 MILES ....

THE ROBIN HOOD WAY — 88 MILES...

DERBYSHIRE —

TRAILS OF NORTH EAST DERBYSHIRE — Five Pits & Rowthorne

BOLSOVER DISTRICT WALK — 6, 15 & 32 MILES ....

DERBYSHIRE BOUNDARY WALK — 280 MILES ....

THE CHESTERFIELD ROUND WALK — 45 MILES ....

DERBYSHIRE GRITSTONE WAY — 56 MILES ....

THE PEAK DISTRICT —

DERWENT WATERSHED WALK — 40 MILES ....

FOUR INNS WALK — 40 MILES...

MARSDEN TO EDALE — 25 MILES ....

THE MASTERS' HIKE — 45 MILES ....

FOUR CIRCULAR WALKS AROUND KINDER AND BLEAKLOW.....

THE RAMBLERS WAY — 38 MILES..

THE LIMEY WAY — 40 MILES..

THE PEAKLAND WAY — 100 MILES ....

THE RIVERS' WAY — 43 MILES ....

PEAKLAND HERITAGE WALK — 36 MILES ....

GRITSTONE EDGE WALK — 23 MILES ....

LIMESTONE DALE WALK — 24 MILES ....

JOHN MERRILL'S PEAK DISTRICT CHALLENGE WALK — 25 MILES ....

THE MINERS' WAY — 68 MILES...

PEAK DISTRICT HIGH LEVEL ROUTE — 90 MILES..........................

DERBYSHIRE TRAILS — Tissington, High Peak, Monsal & Sett Valley...

EIGHT OTHER WALKS...

CHESHIRE —

A CESTRIAN LINK WALK — 120 MILES ....

SANDSTONE TRAIL — 32 MILES...

GRITSTONE TRAIL — 18½ MILES..

THE MIDDLEWOOD WAY — 11 MILES ....

STAFFORDSHIRE —

STAFFORDSHIRE WAY — 90 MILES...

MOW COP TRAIL — 9 MILES..

CANALS — FIVE END TO END WALKS ....